Creative Web Design

with

Adobe®Muse®

David Asch

Focal Press
Taylor & Francis Group

NEW YORK AND LONDON

First published 2014
by Focal Press
70 Blanchard Road, Suite 402, Burlington, MA 01803

Published in the UK
by Focal Press
2 Park Square, Milton Park, Abingdon, Oxon OX14 4RN

Focal Press is an imprint of the Taylor & Francis Group, an informa business

Notices
Knowledge and best practice in this field are constantly changing. As new research and experience broaden our understanding, changes in research methods, professional practices, or medical treatment may become necessary.

Practitioners and researchers must always rely on their own experience and knowledge in evaluating and using any information, methods, compounds, or experiments described herein. In using such information or methods they should be mindful of their own safety and the safety of others, including parties for whom they have a professional responsibility.

Product or corporate names may be trademarks or registered trademarks, and are used only for identification and explanation without intent to infringe.

Library of Congress Cataloging-in-Publication Data
Asch, David.
Creative web design with Adobe Muse / David Asch.
pages cm
ISBN 978-0-415-81179-8 (paperback)
1. Adobe Muse (Electronic resource) 2. Web sites--Authoring programs. 3. Web sites--Design. I. Title.
TK5105.8885.A355A83 2014
006.7'86--dc23
2014008665

ISBN: 978-0-415-81179-8 (pbk)
ISBN: 978-0-203-38522-7 (ebk)

MIX
Paper from
responsible sources
FSC® C014174

Printed and bound in the United States of America by Sheridan Books, Inc. (a Sheridan Group Company).

Table of contents

4 Designing for mobile devices 106

5 Search engine optimization 142

6 Launching the live site 158

7 The left-overs 176

Acknowledgements

This book is dedicated to Josephine, of course, for her support while I wrote it.

Immense thanks to the following people:

Steve Caplin for his continued help and guidance
Donna Ayto from *The Brighton Cake Company*
Dave Bevans, Carlin Bowers, Mary LaMaccia and Denise Power of Focal Press
Technical reviewer, Tommi West

Images used in the book under the Creative Commons licence:

Cover – El Caganger, **Flickr**
Page 4 –Catherine (Sailor Coruscant), **Flickr**
Page 10 – Liz Mc, **Flickr**
Page 44 – Victor Rosenfeld, **Flickr**
Page 106 – Rachel Kramer Bussell, **Flickr**
Page 142 – Daniaphoto, **Fotolia**
Page 158 – Hotzeplotz, **Flickr**
Page 176 – With Associates, **Flickr**

Introduction

Why use Adobe Muse?

Not everyone has the aptitude for building websites using code alone. Typically, the design of the site will be created in Adobe Photoshop (or its equivalent), which is then handed over to the web developer to break down and reconstruct using HTML and CSS. This is fine if your budget supports it but, for many people, this is not an affordable option. Muse gives us the ability to build a site straight from the design concept.

Muse is a totally visual web-design tool. There is no coding needed to put together fully functional websites. Everything is created in a drag and drop environment, Muse handles the code side of the operation, making the design and construction process a whole lot easier for those of us who think CSS is a cable TV channel and Javascript is the receipt you get at the coffee shop.

The visual approach used in Muse will be familiar to anyone who has used a desktop publishing application such as Quark, Adobe InDesign or even Microsoft Publisher. The toolset in Muse is minimal and easy to get to grips with, even if you haven't used similar applications. The fundamental page composition is created using either a text frame or a rectangle. The latter can be simple shapes filled with color, or contain images and even embedded HTML code for video and other rich content. The rest is determined by styling options and widgets: predefined slideshows, menus, forms and presentations.

Who is the book for?

The book is aimed at anyone using Muse for the first time who wants to get stuck in and working from the outset. Rather than looking at the program's features and commands individually, the content is project-based, taking you through the process of putting together a website from start to finish. It is, in fact, based on a working website I created for a local business, *The Brighton Cake Company*, so it is also testament to the program's powerful capabilities. The live site can be found at **www.brightoncakecompany.co.uk**.

There may be differences between the version we're creating here and the live version, this, of course, is one of the downsides of the static printed page versus the ever-evolving Internet. Any major design changes to the site or updates to Muse itself will be detailed on the book's companion website.

There may also be slight changes to some of the design elements used here, compared to the live version, mainly for reasons of intellectual property and privacy but these will be few and far between and are, on the whole, inconsequential to the overall project.

How to use this book

The book is designed primarily to be worked through in a linear fashion, as it runs through from the basics of using Muse up to producing a fully working site. Think of it as a route-map, rather than an atlas; using only the tools and techniques required for the job at hand. It can, however, also be used as a reference book; the chapter intros give an overview of what we'll be doing and there's the index, of course. The format is laid out in a step-by-step style with a screen capture or illustration, along with a caption explaining what's going on.

Although I've attempted to incorporated as many of features of Muse as possible into the site to demonstrate them in context, there are a few that I simply could not shoehorn in without totally disrupting the design and some that were released too late during the writing of the book to be incorporated. For this reason I have placed a chapter at the end of the book with examples of using the features individually.

Keyboard shortcuts

Throughout the book I use a mixture of menu commands and keyboard shortcuts to show how to switch tools and invoke the various features, as some people prefer using one or the other, or sometimes both. It is, however, worth learning the keyboard shortcuts as it can help immensely to speed up the workflow!

The keyboard shortcuts are given for both the Mac and PC platforms where applicable. The format I use is the modifier, **Cmd** and **Opt** for the Mac, **Ctrl** and **Alt** for the PC, followed by the associated keystroke. For example, invoking the **Place** command would be listed like so: **File > Place** (**Cmd+D**/**Ctrl+D**). If the keystroke is the same for both platforms, it is just shown in black, **Shift**, **Tab**, etc. This gives the commands a little more distinction from the rest of the text.

Accompanying website

All the necessary files for putting the example website together are available from the book's accompanying website **www.creativemu.se**. Also, with Adobe's software subscription model, its applications are being updated far more regularly than before. I want to make sure you're kept as up-to-date as possible, of course, so I'll be posting details and tutorials about any new features and changes, along with any other significant news, as and when they happen.

1 Introducing Adobe Muse

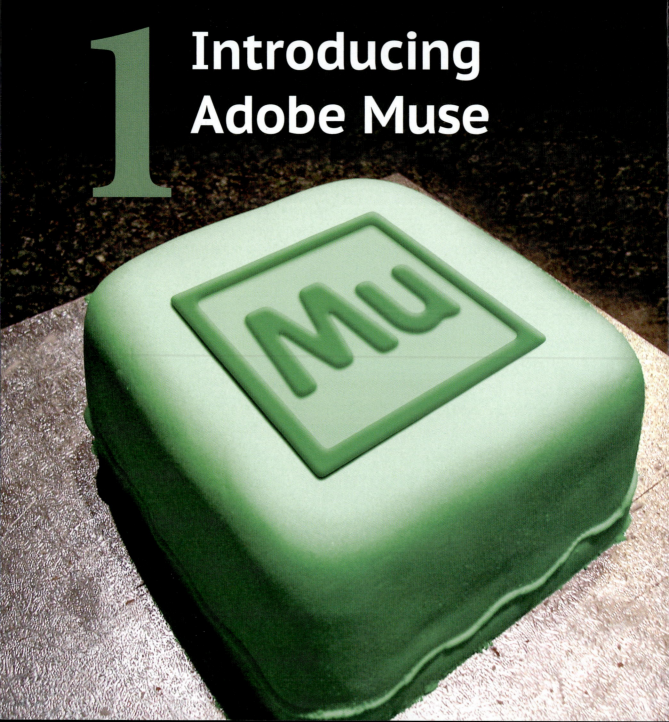

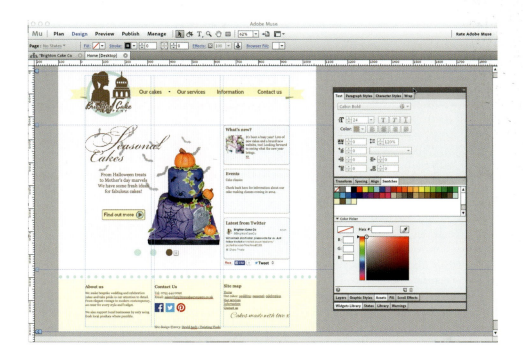

Before we jump in and start building our websites we'll need to familiarize ourselves with Muse and its features. Much of the interface and toolset will be recognizable to you if you've used any of Adobe's applications before. There are a few differences, of course. In this chapter we'll take an overview of the application's features.

Introducing Adobe Muse

Features at a glance

1

We'll be approaching the program as though it has only just been installed. This way we start at the same level, regardless of your previous experience. It's well worth following from the beginning, even if you have used the program before; there's always something that you might have missed.

The Welcome Screen

As with most of the Creative Cloud applications, when we first launch Muse, the first thing we see is the Welcome screen.

On the left we have the options to create a new site and also to open any recent sites we have been working on, this is empty at the moment, as we're yet to create any.

On the right are links to online learning resources and to interact with the Muse community. These all require an active Internet connection; as this is a web-design program, it's highly likely you already have one of those, of course!

We can also choose to prevent the dialog from opening each time by checking the box in the bottom-left corner. The dialog will remain visible until we choose an action but will no longer show when Muse is launched. This is personal preference, of course; I prefer not to have it showing. If you later decide you do want it showing, it can be toggled in the program preferences. It's also possible to start new sites and open recent ones from the menus.

Creating a new site

The next step is to start off our new site project. To do this we can click the **Create New > Site** button. This opens the New Site dialog; we can also invoke this by choosing **Create New > Site** if we opted to not display the welcome dialog.

Here we can choose the initial layout type from Desktop, Tablet or Phone. Each preset has a default set of values based on the standard sizes for their respective devices. These can also be set manually, of course and will not be overridden when reselecting the preset.

We would generally have an idea of the layout beforehand and could set the values

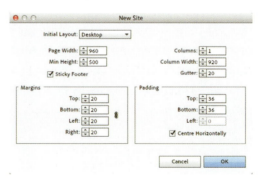

The dimensions and layout of the site can be set initially using the New Site dialog.

up now. For the purposes of this chapter, however, we'll leave the dialog at its defaults; they can be edited at any time once we are in the main working area. Clicking **OK** takes us into the **Plan mode**.

It's also possible to bypass the dialog altogether by holding **Opt**/**Alt** when clicking the option to start a new site on the welcome dialog.

Working in Plan mode

Plan mode is where the layout of the site is created and controlled. This has two sections, the site map at the top and the master page view at the bottom. When we create a new site, we always start with a Home page and a Master page (named *A-Master* by default). If you've worked with Adobe InDesign, the concept of master pages will be familiar; these generally contain the site assets that are going to be consistent across the site. These will often be the header and footer components, site navigation and background color or pattern. Many sites will only need one master, whereas others may have several, depending on the design. It's also possible to create master pages that inherit only certain traits of their peers, such as the footer elements, giving us more design options, whilst keeping the overall theme and ease of use.

We can open several sites at once, they appear as tabs at the top of the workspace. This can be useful if we want to copy previously used elements from one site to another. Do bear in mind that this may decrease the performance of the program.

Once we start creating pages, we can choose the order in which they appear, add and remove pages and also organize the pages at different levels to create a hierarchy; Muse can automatically generate the site navigation based on this layout. All this will become clear as we progress through the chapters.

Production modes
Use these buttons to switch between the five program modules.

Thumbnail controls
Change how the page thumbnails are displayed

Layout options
These switch between the desktop and alternate mobile layout designs.

Site map
This is the 'canvas' for creating the site.

Page thumbnail
The individual pages that make up the site.

Master pages
These form the basis that define the shared design elements of the site.

Master page indicators
The blue labels display the currently assigned master page on the site pages, and the inherited master(s) for the master pages.

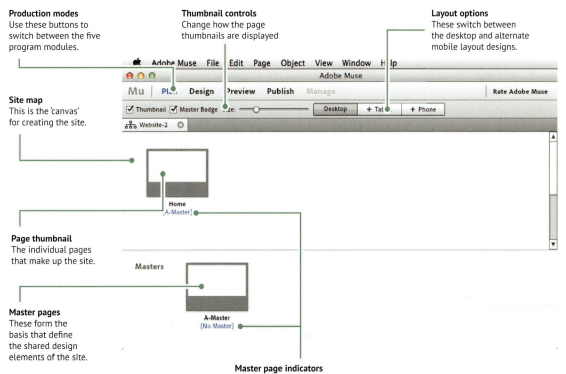

1 Introducing Adobe Muse

Design mode

Design mode is where the page building happens. All text, images and special content (Photoshop buttons, rectangles, widgets, and embedded HTML) is created here. To open a page into this view, we double-click its thumbnail in the Plan mode. The screenshot below shows a master page in the workspace.

Unlike other Creative Cloud programs, the toolset in Muse is minimal and resides at the top of the window, rather than being within the workspace itself. Below the toolbar is the Control panel. This displays the settings and options relating to the currently selected object in the design.

Just below the Control Panel is the tab area. As with the Plan mode, we can have several pages open at once, each being represented by a tab with the page title. In Muse, windows cannot be separated from the tab bar, as they can in other applications.

The main workspace has three areas. The lighter gray area is the application background. The darker gray represents the browser fill: the area around the page content that stretches to fill the window when the page is viewed in the web browser. The white area is the page or master page content.

Around the workspace are the rulers, the measurements are in pixels. The rulers can be toggled on and off from the View menu and the View Options menu in the Control panel, or by right-clicking on the rulers themselves.

The large floating dock on the right contains panels with the settings for each tool and object. Some mirror those available in the Control panel and top-level menus, others can only be accessed from the panel. The individual panels can be moved between sections in the dock and toggled on or off but cannot be dragged out independently. The whole dock can be collapsed down to a single column of icons to free up space.

Toolbar
The tools for designing pages

Control panel
Settings for the currently active object

Page content
The visible area of the page design

Browser fill
Displays the content of the site's background

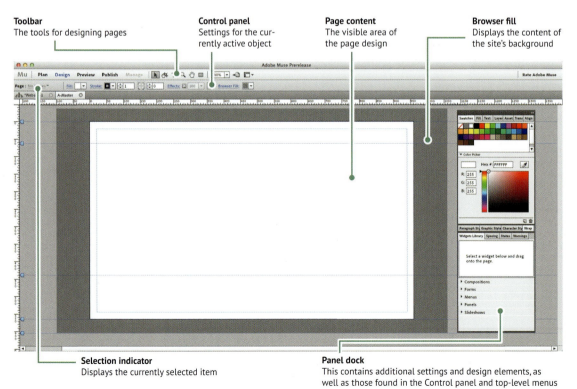

Selection indicator
Displays the currently selected item

Panel dock
This contains additional settings and design elements, as well as those found in the Control panel and top-level menus

Preview mode

Preview mode displays the currently active page rendered as it will appear in the browser. Everything works as it should, including site navigation and any externally referenced page content such as embedded video.

The initial page generation can be a little slower than it is when viewed in a browser, particularly when navigating the site for the first time or if the content has changed since the last view. Subsequent previews will be much faster.

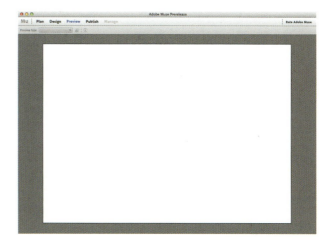

Publish mode

Technically, this is not a window view and is only applicable to Muse trial sites and if you choose to fully host the site through Adobe.

A standalone Muse subscription comes with one trial site, subscription to the full Creative Cloud edition has five sites.

When selected, a dialog appears with the existing live or trial site details, or the option to create a new site. Once published, the live version of the trial site is displayed in a new browser window.

Manage

Again, this is only available for trial sites and live sites hosted by Adobe. Clicking the Manage option opens a browser window and logs in to the Muse Dashboard.

This gives you access to, amongst other things, hosting details such as space and bandwidth use, site reports and also access to the in-browser editing system.

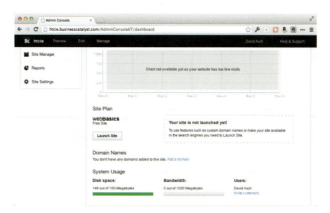

2 Designing the master page

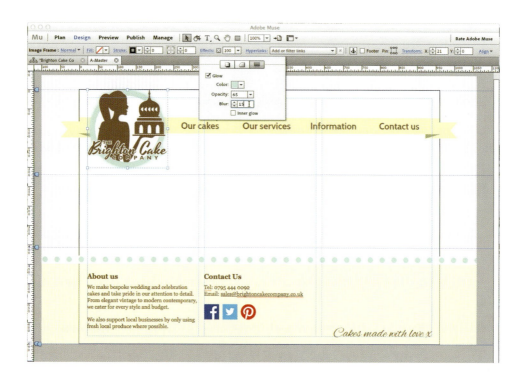

We're ready to start designing the website. Before we begin, however, we'll need to have an idea of not only what it's going to look like but also how it will flow, to determine its ease-of-use to the person using it. Although it is possible to jump in and create the layout on-the-fly in Muse, it's not recommended, as it can lead to an unstructured and messy design that could take longer to fix than it did to create. That's not something either the designer or the client would want.

2 Designing the master page
Planning the site

As with any type of design, communication between the designer and their client is paramount. This ensures that he or she is getting the site they want but are also aware of the limitations of what is possible, either within Muse or more generally on the web itself.

The initial site layout

It's likely that your client may already have a website, as was the case with *The Brighton Cake Company*; they had used one of the many online out-of-the-box services (**Figs. 1, 2 & 3**). Whilst this meant that they could quickly have a presence on the web without having a site professionally built for them, these online resources can often be restrictive in the way they are put together. What it meant, however, is we had something to work with at the start of the process. This is good because, as designers, we can get a feel of how the client wants the color schemes and general content. We won't always have this luxury, of course!

fig 1. The landing page

fig 2. Product gallery

fig 3. Information about the company's wedding cake service.

Once we have an idea of the basic structure and the colors the client wants, we can move on to putting our new site together. The first step is generally to sketch out a rough idea on paper – often the back of an envelope – before we transcribe it onto something more formal to show the client. This is the wire-frame model. The site's layout is represented as a series of boxes, sometimes drawn freehand but more often placed on a grid.

If, like me, your freehand drawing skills are lacking, there are many applications available to aid the wireframing process. There are many free web-based and desktop tools out there. You could also use Muse itself to create the wireframe mock-ups, of course.

Once the wire-frame has been defined, a more complex preview can be created, most likely in a graphics application such as Adobe Photoshop. This time we would be using draft versions of images and proper text, whether that's *Lorem Ipsum* place-holder text or the actual text being used for the site. This enables color schemes and typefaces to be tested out in readiness to create the final version.

Normally, at this stage, we would slice up the flat design and pass the images over to a web-developer to code everything in to the working site. Not with Muse at hand, of course. Once we have our images we can start building the site straight onto the page. If you have Photoshop CC, it's well worth using its Generator feature to output the images. It's far easier than using the traditional slice tool.

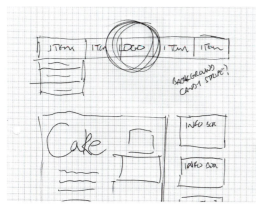

Sketching on graph paper makes it easier to transfer the design to the grid-based web layout.

Muse can be used as a wireframing tool as well!

The final design in Adobe Photoshop.

Designing the master page
Preparing the new site

The site properties

With the basis of the site design drawn out and translated into its component images we can begin to construct it in Muse. As we saw in the introduction, we can do this either from the welcome screen or from within the program by selecting New Site from the File menu (shortcut: **Cmd+N/ Ctrl+N**). This opens the **New Site** dialog.

The content in our site design has been made to the standard 960 pixel width, so we can leave the dimensions at their defaults; the height can be controlled visually once we're in the design module. It's worth noting at this stage that the width and height settings only determine the width of the content area, not the entire site.

Below the page dimensions is the **Sticky Footer** option. This prevents the footer from floating up the page where the browser's height is greater than the page content. This is especially useful when setting up the site for mobile devices as it maintains a uniform layout. The option can be set independently for each version of the site, if we need the pages to behave differently on each. Generally, we'd leave it enabled.

We'll set the number of columns to 3, as this suits our layout. As we do, Muse automatically sets the column width in accordance to the width of the page and the size of the gutter. The default 20 pixel gutter is a little wide, so we'll drop that to 15. Again, Muse updates the column width.

The margins, as in most publishing applications, determine the offset amount of the content relative to the page width. This won't be evident in our design as the content is floating on the background and can be left at the default of 20 pixels. Be more mindful of the margins when designing sites with a page content background that's different to the browser fill.

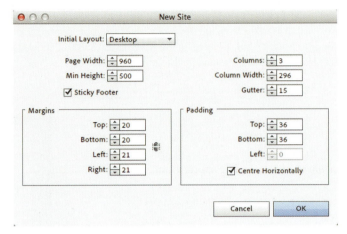

Padding determines how much space is left between the top and bottom of the browser window, again, we'll leave this at the defaults. **Center Horizontally** makes sure the content is in the middle of the browser at all times.

960px is a good width for a basic website.

Now we have the basics of the layout set up, we can click **OK** accept the settings and close the New Site dialog. We're now taken into the **Plan mode** where we can begin setting up the default master page and start working on the content.

Save your work!

Now would be a good time to save our new site. From the File Menu choose Save. We'll name it *Brighton Cake Co.muse*. It's also worth noting that Muse autosaves as we progress, so if the program crashes, or there's a power-cut, we will rarely lose too much of our work. It's also good practice to manually save as we go along, just in case!

Designing the master page

When we first enter the **Plan mode** in Muse, it looks a little sparse. We have a single thumbnail representing the *Home* page in the site layout area and an, as yet, undefined master page. The default master is named *A-Master* and is applied to the home page (denoted by the blue label below the page name). Neither pages have any content at the moment, so they appear blank. The order in which we start working on the site depends on personal preference. I tend to start by setting up the master page elements, this gives me a better feel of how the pages will look before I move on to creating the site layout. You may decide to do this the other way round. There is no right or wrong approach.

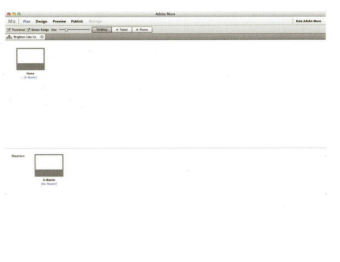

▶ To start editing the page, double-click its thumbnail. This brings us into the **Design mode**. This will look familiar to anyone who's used a desktop publishing application. The page content is represented by the rectangle in the center, as we would expect to find with a print-design layout. We can see the guides and margins we set up in the New Site dialog.

There's one big difference between a layout in Muse and a traditional DTP application. Muse uses a flexible layout: we can adjust the size of the page and the distance between the page and the top and bottom of the browser window. This can be done initially within the master page to set the site standard but can be altered on a page-by-page basis to suit the content of each. All this is done visually by dragging the horizontal guides on the left of the window. We'll look at this in more detail as we progress through the chapter.

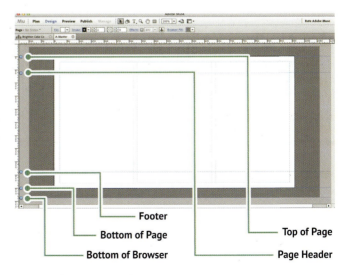

Footer

Bottom of Page

Bottom of Browser

Top of Page

Page Header

Setting the browser fill

The default browser fill is an drab shade of gray. To change this, go to the **Control Panel** at the top of the window and click **Browser Fill**. This opens the Browser Fill options panel. Currently it's set to a solid fill. We also have the option to use a gradient. This site uses a graphic background fill. Click the folder icon next to where it says **Image**. A file browser dialog opens. Navigate to where you saved the assets for the chapter. Select the *light-stripes.jpg* file. Click **Open**.

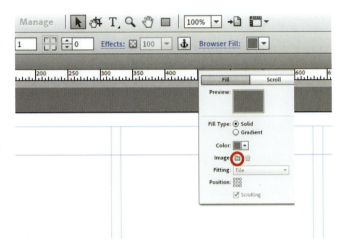

The **Fitting** type is already set to **Tile** in the example, this fills the background with an image that tiles both horizontally and vertically. This is what we need here but we have several other options to choose from, depending on the layout we want:

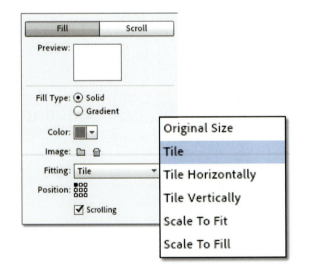

- **Original size** displays the image you select once on the page at its original dimensions, and aligns the image based on the selected **Position** option.

- **Tile Horizontally** repeats the image in a single row across the page. Its alignment is defined by the **Position** selector.

- **Tile Vertically** does the same as Tile Horizontally but creates a single column of tiled images.

- **Scale To Fit** displays the chosen image proportionally to fit the browser background. This can result in gaps around the image, depending on its ratio and starting position.

- **Scale To Fill** displays the chosen image so it always fills the browser background. Areas around the edges of the image may be clipped, so it's important that nothing of importance is placed there.

The **Scrolling** option at the bottom of the panel determines whether the background image will scroll with the page if it's too large for the browser window, or remain fixed, while the page content scrolls above it. With a patterned background like this, we can leave it checked. Fixed backgrounds can affect the site's performance, particularly with photographs and large amounts of page content.

You can choose how your background image fill displays in the browser fill area.

▶ Here's how the page looks so far. We now have the striped background filling the browser fill area, with the white page area in the center; this won't be filled in the final version but we'll keep it solid for now, as it acts as a guide to assist with the alignment of the page elements.

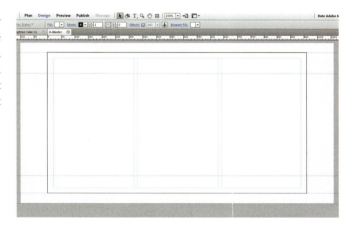

▶ There are two control guides at the top of the workspace. This first guide sets the top of the page. This sets the amount of space between the top of the visible content and the edge of the browser window area (where we see the browser fill in our design). The default is **36px** – as it was set in the padding section of the site properties – which is enough breathing space, so we'll leave it where it is.

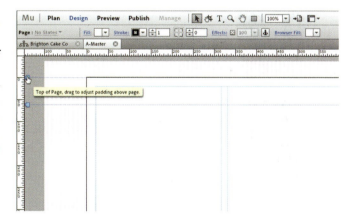

Define the header

Now we'll set the **Header guide** to define the area where the header elements be placed. The height of header design is **200px** and we'll need a margin between the header and the page content. Drag the guide down to **220px**. This gives us an initial gap of **20px**. We can always alter it at a later time, of course; Muse will automatically shift the content of the pages accordingly.

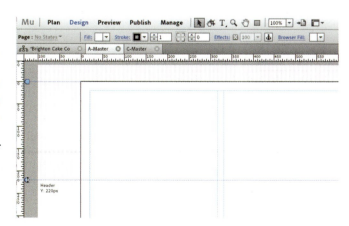

2 Designing the master page

Add the header images

Choose **File > Place** (keyboard shortcut **Cmd+D/Ctrl+D**). Again, this will be familiar to InDesign users. A file dialog opens up. Browse to the *Chapter 2* Assets folder and select *logo.png*. Click **Open**. This has loaded the **Place tool** with the first part of our header graphic. We can see a small representation of it hanging off the cursor. The dotted right-angle on the left of the cursor represents the top corner of the image to be placed. This helps us to position the graphic element if it's an irregular shape.

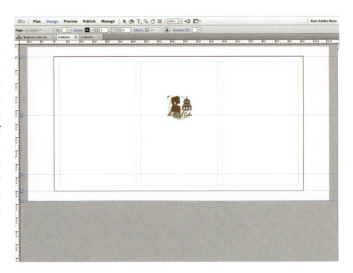

▶ Click once to set the image down; this places our logo graphic at full size. Click inside the image's bounding box with the **Selection tool (V)**. Drag the image up to the top of the content area until it snaps into place; the horizontal guide turns red to show it's aligned to the top of the page.

Now drag it toward the center of the page. When we hit dead center we not only see a red guide to tell us we are at the center, we also see these two blue bars with pixel values. These indicate that the object is equally positioned between two other objects – the center column guides in this instance.

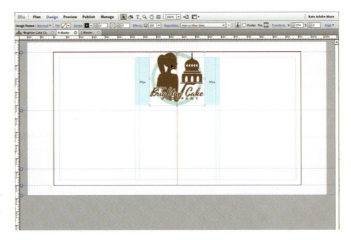

▶ Next we'll add the ribbon graphic that will eventually hold the site's main navigation menu.

Go to **File > Place**. Select the file *ribbon.png* to load it into the **Place tool**. Click once as we did before to set it down at full size on the page. Again, don't worry about the positioning at the moment, we'll be looking at a quick way to align objects in the next section.

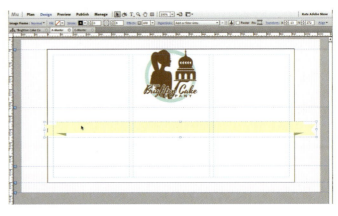
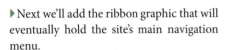

The alignment tools

We're going to align the ribbon to the logo. Grab the **Selection tool** if it's not already active. Click once on the logo image. Now hold down the **Shift** key and click the ribbon image. Release **Shift**. Both items are now selected. It's important that we do this in the correct order.

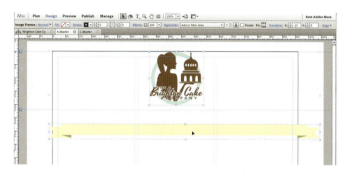

▶ Go to the **Control panel**. Click **Align** to open the **Alignment options panel** – the same options are also available in the docked panel set. We have the usual alignment tools available to us. Before we start, however, we need to tell Muse what we want the objects to align to – the logo in this instance.

Click the **Align to** button to open its options. Select **Align to Key Object**. The key object is the first item in a multi-selection, hence the importance of selecting the objects in order. A heavy dotted frame appears around the logo.

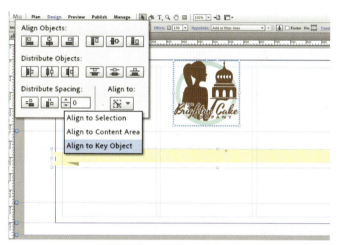

▶ Click the **Align Horizontal Centers** button in the **Align Objects** section of the **Alignment options panel**. The ribbon snaps into place, in line with the logo.

▶ Now click the **Align Vertical Centers** button to bring the ribbon up to the center of the logo. We can deselect the objects now by clicking away from them on the page, or by going to **Edit > Deselect All**.

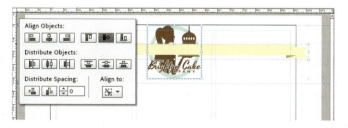

2 Designing the master page

▶ Finally, for this stage of the design, we need to change the order of the objects to bring the logo in front of the ribbon. Click the logo image to select it again. Now go to **Object > Bring to Front**. We can also right-click and choose **Arrange > Bring to Front** in the menu that appears.

Build the footer

The footer is where the company's brief mission statement appears, as well as at-a-glance contact details and social media links. We'll start by increasing the minimum page size: drag the **Bottom of Page guide** down to **650px**. This will give us some breathing space when it comes to building the page content.

The Rectangle tool

Grab the **Rectangle tool** (**M**). Position the cursor on the intersection of the far left of the browser area (not the page edge) and the **Bottom of page guide**. Click and drag out a frame with a height of **210px** over to the right of edge the browser area. As we hit the right edge we see a red guide appear. This denotes that the rectangle will always display at 100% width; the live guide display also shows this.

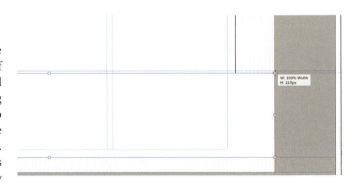

▶ Next, we'll set the color of the footer rectangle. We'll be using the same color as the header ribbon so make sure it's visible in the window. Open the **Fill options**. Click the **Fill Color** swatch to open the color picker. Click the **Sample Color** tool. Now click on the header ribbon to sample its color.

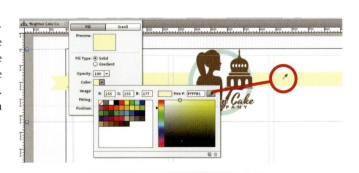

▶The color is a little strong and could be distracting. We could choose a lighter version of the color, of course, but I decided to reduce the **Opacity** instead. Set the **Fill Opacity** to **50**. This gives us a softer pastel shade and allows a little of the background texture to show through as well. Close the panel by clicking the **Fill** link again.

▶Rectangles in Muse always have a 1 pixel black stroke set by default. We don't need it here. We can do this by setting the Stroke value to **0**.

▶Now let's create the decorative divider. Make sure the **Rectangle tool** is selected. Drag out a rectangle from one side of the browser area to the other as before, making sure the red guides appear to denote it's 100% width. Set the height to **21px**.

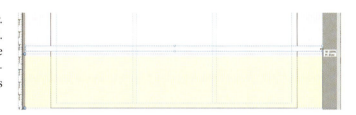

▶Grab the **Selection tool** (**V**). Hold **Shift** to constrain the direction of movement. Now click and drag the rectangle down until it snaps into place above the box we just created. The red guide we can see here is where the rectangle is straddling the Footer guide.

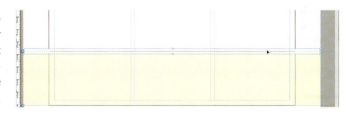

▶Now we'll style the divider. Open the **Fill options** on the **Control panel**. Click the image folder to show the file dialog. Select the *dot.jpg* file.

Although the rectangle is the same height as the graphic, we'll set the **Fitting** to **Tile Horizontal**. This way, if we decide to make the band wider at any point, we'll still only get one row of dots. We can leave the position pin where it is. As before, we also need to remove the default stroke by setting its value to **0**.

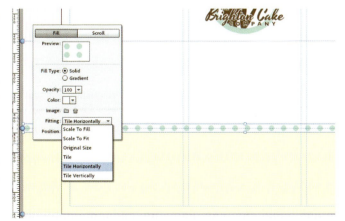

2 Designing the master page

▶ Before we move on to adding the footer content, we need to make a couple of final adjustments. We need to move the **Footer guide** up to include a margin area, as we did with the header. The top of the divider is at **427px**. Move the guide up to **408px** to give us the same 20 pixel margin as the header.

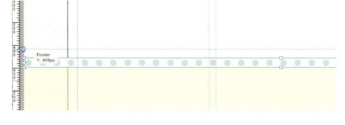

▶ We also have some space below the footer. This means there will be a gap between the footer and the bottom of the browser window. Drag the **Bottom of browser guide** up to meet the **Bottom of Page guide**.

Create the footer content

Our first text frame is going to be the company's brief introduction. Grab the **Text tool** (shortcut: **T**). Position the cursor on the left-hand page margin, a little way down from the divider – around the same distance as is between the **Bottom of Page guide** and the base of the content area. Click and drag the bounding box out to meet the opposite corner of the first column; it should snap into place as we near it. Release the mouse to set the text frame in place.

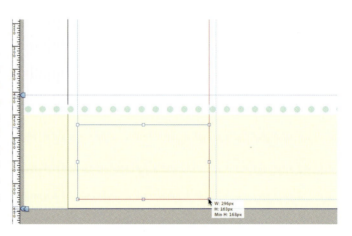

▶ The text for the first panel in the footer is in the chapter's Assets folder (*About us.rtf*). Open it up in TextEdit or Notepad. Copy the text to the clipboard. Now go back to Muse. Click the cursor inside the first text frame. Now go to **Edit > Paste** to populate the box. We need to style the text, of course. As we'll see in the next section, Muse gives us a lot of control over the formatting of text on the page.

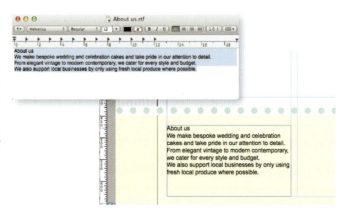

Setting a typeface

Select the **Text panel** from the docked panel set. The first thing we'll look at is the font options. Click the drop-down menu at the top. Here, the list of typefaces is broken down into three categories.

- **Web Safe** fonts are installed by default on every computer platform, so it's assumed that if you use a typeface from this set, it will be rendered the same for everyone visiting the website. The problem with this is we don't have much in the way of variety, so the design options are fairly limited.

- **System** fonts installed on your computer. Whilst they can all be used in your Muse designs, there's no guaranteed that the visitor will have the font installed and it may be substituted for a different typeface. This can ruin the site's layout. For this reason, when system fonts are used, they're converted to images when you publish the site. This keeps the design true to the original but can result in slower loading times if they're used liberally, not to mention the detrimental effect to search-engine ranking; image-based text won't be read by search engines. You should also avoid system fonts where text might need to be selected and copied by the user, such as addresses and phone numbers. If you do need to use a system font, it's best to keep it minimal for headings.

- **Web fonts** have been created to overcome the limitations of the two previous methods of using text on the web. Rather than being installed on the computer, web fonts are downloaded when the page is opened and cached so we can create rich typography-oriented sites that are rendered in real-time.

Spoilt for choice

Currently there are 400+ typefaces available to us with the Muse/Creative Cloud subscription, giving a far greater scope to what we can create. It is worth noting, however, that use of web fonts can also slow down the page loading time, as each of the font families used in the design has to be downloaded in their entirety to allow for the different styles, regardless of whether they are actually used in the design. Adobe suggests using only 1-2 different font families per site.

Styling text

As well as the fonts themselves, Muse has many design-based layout features for text. There are the usual size, weight and style settings, along with the alignment options, including Align Justified. We also have great positional control with tracking, leading, first line indent, space before and after and indent options.

We also have the option to create paragraph and character styles. This gives us much greater control, as we can change the style of headings and body text once and have the changes reflected right across the site. Styles can also be set to use web standard features such as heading tags for search engine optimization and additional formatting options like subscript and superscript and other such display styles. We'll be looking at these features in more depth later on in the book.

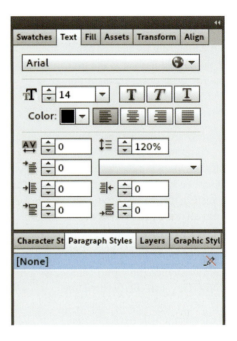

▶Now we have an overview of using type, let's apply styling to the text we just added. We'll start off by adjusting the heading.

Highlight the words *About Us*. We'll be using the web-standard *Georgia* typeface for the footer, so select it from the font menu – I'm using the settings in the docked panels here but, as before, we could also use the font options in the **Control panel**. I've set the size to **18pt** and the weight to **bold**.

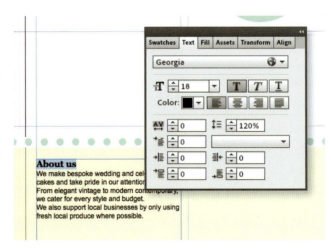

About us
We make bespoke wedding and cel
cakes and take pride in our attention
From elegant vintage to modern contemporary,
we cater for every style and budget.
We also support local businesses by only using
fresh local produce where possible.

▶ Next we'll set the color of the text. For this we'll use the chocolate brown from the company logo. Scroll up or zoom out if you can't currently see the header graphic. Click on the color swatch to open the color picker. Use the **Sample Color** tool to select the brown from the logo.

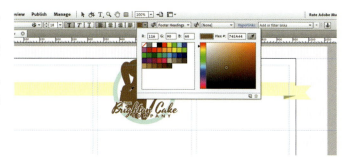

▶ Whilst we have the picker open, we can create a new swatch preset. This will save time when we need to use this color elsewhere in the site and will also enable us to change every instance where the color is used in a single action.

Click the **New Swatch** icon in the bottom-right corner to create a new swatch. At present it's named with the color value. We can change this. Double-click the new swatch to open the **Swatch Options** dialog. Click into the **Swatch Name** field. Type in *Chocolate Brown*. As we do, the **Name with Color value** box is automatically unchecked.

Click **OK** to save the changes. This will make it easier to find later on. The swatch preset is site-wide so the new color will be available for other design elements, too.

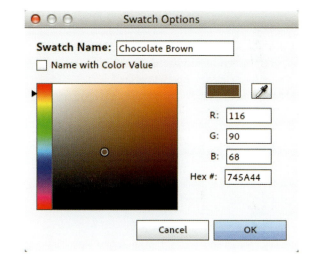

▶ The last bit of styling we'll do to the heading is to add a buffer space below to give it a little separation from the body text. We'll do this by adjusting the **Space After** setting in the **Text panel**. A value of **8px** is adequate here; the body text below is pushed down so there's no need to create a separate text box to achieve the same result.

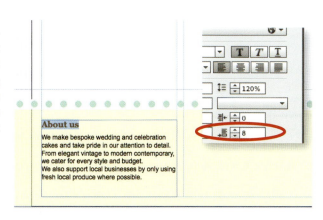

Designing the master page

2

▶ Now for the body text. As with the heading, we'll start by selecting the whole of the text. Go back to the **Text panel**. The list in the font menu now has an additional section titled Recently Used Fonts. As we've only used *Georgia* so far, it's the only one showing up. Click it to apply the typeface to the selected text.

▶ The color will be the same as the header. We can now pick it from the **Swatch panel**. Select the *Chocolate Brown* preset we created earlier in the chapter.

▶ The default font size of **14px** suits the text here so we'll leave it there. We can add a hard return to create a separate paragraph for the bottom line of the text, just to make it cleaner.

Create a paragraph style

Before we move on to the rest of the footer content, we can take a look at creating paragraph styles based on the text we've already created. First let's set a style for the header.

Highlight the header text again; it doesn't need to be the whole line, as we're only sampling the styling we used.

Open the **Paragraph Styles panel**; if it's not visible, choose **Window > Paragraph Styles** to display it. Currently the only entry is the default *[None]* item. Click the **New Style** icon in the bottom-right corner. A new entry named *Paragraph Style* appears in the list.

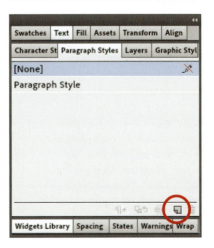

▶ Obviously we need to change the name to something a little more descriptive; it might be the only style we have now but after designing a sites, we could very easily have dozens of different styles defined.

Double-click on the new style to open the **Style Options** dialog box. Here we can change the style name and set the paragraph tag. For now, we'll only set the name. *Footer Headings* is a decent enough description.

The rest of the dialog shows us the style details. We can see the associated size, color, font and the Space After setting we applied. This is information only and cannot be edited.

Click **OK** to save the name change. Now repeat the process using a sample of the body text. We can call this *Footer Body*, in line with our naming convention.

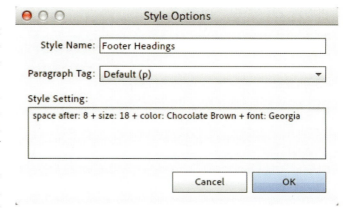

▶ Create another text frame aligned to the top of the previous frame. Drag the side handles until they snap to the center column guides to set the width. Open up the file *Contact Us.rtf*. Copy the contents into the new frame as we did before. The squiggly red lines under words that are seen as potential spelling errors highlighted by the built-in spell-checker. Highlight the *Contact Us* heading. Go over to the **Paragraph Styles panel**. Click the *Footer Headings* style. This applies the same attributes as the previous heading. We can select the telephone number and the email and apply the *Footer Body* style.

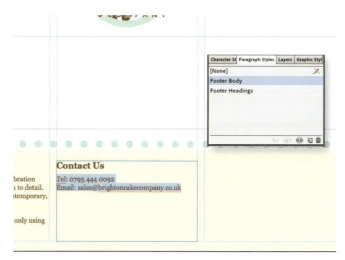

Create an email link

We can make the email address a hyperlink, of course. Select just the email address. Go to the **Edit menu** and select **Copy** (or press **Cmd+C**/**Ctrl+C**). Muse will automatically check to see if it can resolve the address from an internal site link. If it can't find one, it asks us to press **Enter** and it will generate a new external link.

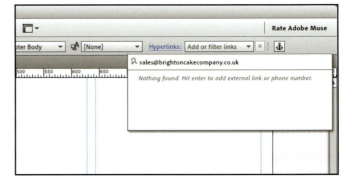

▶ Muse has recognized that we are creating an email link and has added the necessary HTML mailto prefix to enable browsers to launch the computer's default mail client when the link is clicked. We have a problem, however; although the link's typeface has been retained, Muse has used the default link colors – bright blue for an unvisited link, – overriding our custom paragraph style. We'll need to create a new link style for email links.

▶ Like paragraph and character styles, hyperlink styles are set globally. Curiously, however, they are not found alongside the others. Instead we need to open the **Hyperlink Options panel** in the **Control panel** and click the **Edit Link Styles** button. We can make the same changes by choosing **File > Site Properties** and clicking the **Content** tab.

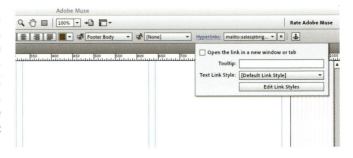

Create a link style

Here's the **Content panel** open in the **Site Properties** window. Currently we only see the default style and its associated settings. We'll leave that as it is. Click the **New Style** icon just below the styles list. We now have an entry named *[Default Link Style] copy*. This is misleading as it's not a copy, it's a new style. We can rename this by double-clicking the name. Name it *Footer Email*.

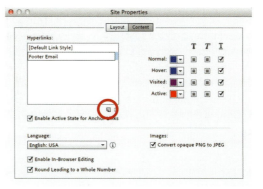

▶Let's look at the settings we have to control the link appearance in more detail. There are four potential states. The first is **Normal**. This determines how the link appears on the page, without the visitor having hovered over it or previously visited it.

● The first setting is the link state's color. This opens the color picker. We'll make it a slightly darker brown so it stands out without being too blatant: the swatch next to our custom swatch is good.

● The next setting determines if the link is bold or not. This has three states. The default, denoted by a square, is to use the existing styling of the original text. Clicking on it gives us a check mark. This means the link will always be bold, regardless of the original styling. Clicking again clears the box. This tells Muse never to make the link bold. Generally, we'll stick with the default setting of inheriting the original style.

● Following on we have settings to make the text to italics and to set its underline styling. Again, these each have the same three options as the bold state. We'll leave the italics set to inherit. The default setting for the underline style is to always underline, which we'll use here.

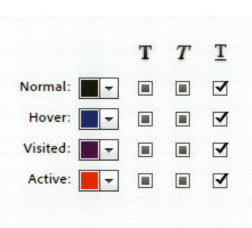

▶ Now we have styled the **Normal** state, we can go through the rest of the settings to finish off the custom link style. Next in the list is the **Hover** state. This, as we would expect, determines how the link will appear when a visitor hovers their cursor over it. We'll keep our email link simple by setting the Hover style to the same color as before but take away the underline so it's visibly doing something when the cursor is over it. To do this, we click once on the under-line setting.

▶ The next state is **Visited**. For standard page links it's useful to set a different style for this, as it lets the visitor know that they have previously used the link. For mail links, however, it's not really nec-essary. We'll set the styling the same as the **Normal** state, so we just need to change the color.

▶ The final state is **Active**. This determines the appearance of the link when it's clicked. As it's only seen in one instance, let's make it a little more noticeable. I've sampled the *Mint Green* from the row of dots in the footer – it's a good time to create another custom swatch, too – as that will be a good contrasting accent to show the visitor they've clicked the link. I've also turned the underline off to match the hover state.

▶ Click **OK** to save the changes. Although we had the email selected when we created the new style, it hasn't been applied because Muse doesn't know we wanted it assigned to the link. To do this, go back to the **Hyperlink Options** in the **Control panel**. Click the **Text Link Style** drop-down and choose the new *Footer Email* style.

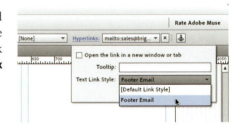

Be careful with your styles!

It's tempting to want to drastically change the appearance of the different link states by making them italic or bold, or both. Remember that in doing so, you are increasing the size of the type, so it may well force both the link and any surrounding elements onto a new line, which isn't at all pretty!

Links don't need to be text-based, of course, they can be applied to almost any of the design elements in Muse; we'll be seeing this in action later in the book. The next part of the project is to add some social media buttons into the contact section. Muse has a great feature for doing this called Place Photoshop Button. This allows us to open a Photoshop PSD file and use its individual layers to determine the states of the button.

Working with Photoshop buttons

We'll start by creating the Facebook button. Go to **File > Place Photoshop Button** or use the keyboard shortcut **Cmd+B/Ctrl+B**. A file dialog opens. Browse to the *Chapter 2* assets folder. Find the *Facebook.psd* file. Click **Open**. Instead of giving us an image on the Place gun as we had when we added graphic elements before, the **Photoshop Import Options** dialog box appears.

The PSD file has four layers, each of which can be assigned to a particular link state; the drop-down menus next to each state show us the names of the layers. I've used the same colors for the Rollover and Mouse Down states as we set for the email link. The Normal and Active states are the same as we need it to show the correct colors by default. Click **OK** to apply and close the dialog.

▶ We're back to the standard Place gun with the Facebook button loaded. I've saved the buttons at their correct size so we can click once underneath the text to add it to the page. I've left a reasonable margin between the text and the buttons here. The edge of the icon is aligned the left side to the edge of the text frame. Repeat the process for the Twitter and Pinterest buttons. We can use the Spacing guides to make sure the buttons are equally distributed.

▶ We need to tell Muse where these buttons will link to, of course! We'll start with the *Pinterest* button, as it's currently selected. The URLs are listed in the *Social Media Links.rtf* file in the *Chapter 2* assets folder. Select the link text and copy it to the clipboard. Now go up to the **Control panel** and click the **Hyperlink** drop-down. Paste the Pinterest link in to assign it to the button. Repeat this for *Facebook* and *Twitter* buttons.

Open the **Hyperlink options** in the **Control panel**. Enable the option **Open the link in a new window or tab**; this ensures that the visitor doesn't leave the site. We can also add some tooltip text. This appears when you hover over the button. Something like *Find us on Facebook!*, *Twitter*, etc.

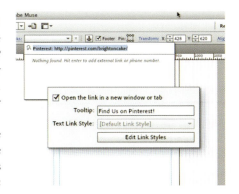

2 Designing the master page

The final part of the footer is to add the company's slogan. We'll use another text frame but this time, we'll use a decorative font; it's a good opportunity to take a look at working with the web fonts available to us through the Muse and Creative Cloud subscription.

Working with Web Fonts

Select the **Text tool**. Draw out a text frame at the bottom of the final column, spanning its entire width. Click **Add Web Fonts** in the font menu of the **Text panel**. A new window appears, it may take a short time to populate at first as it needs to create the cached list of fonts.

At the top of the window is the filter bar. Here we can narrow down the list of fonts by name; this is a wildcard search, so terms like Script, Regular, etc. all work. We can also narrow the list by category. Next we have two buttons: the first displays typefaces for headings, the second is for body text. The check mark at the end filters the font or fonts that are currently selected.

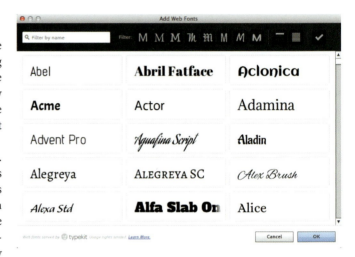

▶ To add the font, *Alex Brush* in this instance, simply click the entry in the main window and click **OK**. A message appears to tell you that it's been added to the Web Fonts menu (this can be turned off if it becomes annoying). Open the font list again and there's our chosen font ready to use. Click the entry to make it the active font.

▶ Go to the **Text panel**. Set the font size to **35**. Open the **Swatch presets** and select the *Chocolate Brown* preset. We want the slogan to butt against the right of the frame, so set the **Alignment** to **Right** by clicking its button. Now we can type in the slogan: *Cakes made with love x*.

Nudge the text frame with the **Selection tool** by pressing **Left** and **Right Arrow keys**, so the slogan is sitting on the very bottom of the text frame.

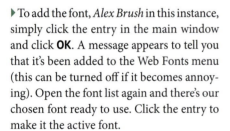

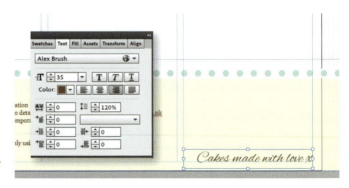

The master page is almost complete. The final stage is to add the main site navigation. Before we do this, we should really add some more pages to our site plan. We can also take the opportunity to see how the master will look when viewed as a web page. Just in case anything goes awry, save the site before we move on (we've also been doing this periodically during the design process, of course!).

Preview the page

Click the **Preview mode** button at the top of the Muse window. A progress bar appears as it gathers the components together in order to render them as a working web page. This may take a little while the first time as it has to cache the components; subsequent pre-view renders will be a lot faster, depending on how much is changed in between. We can see how the footer extends to fill the width of the browser. It looks a little odd as we still have the white content but we'll be removing that.

Add new pages

Go back to the **Plan mode**. We can see the Home page thumbnail has now updated to reflect the work we've done on the master design. We'll add some more pages to the site, based on the draft layout.

Hover over the *Home* page thumbnail. We see three plus signs and a cross appear around it. The plus signs give us the option to add pages to the left, right or below the currently selected page, the cross, as you'd expect, will delete the page.

The position in the **Plan mode** determines how the pages appear on the navigation menus by default, this can be overridden, of course. We'll add a new page to the right by clicking the right-hand button. The new page automatically assumes the design of the master page. The page title is high-lighted so we'll change it to *Our Cakes*, as this will be the first page in the menu.

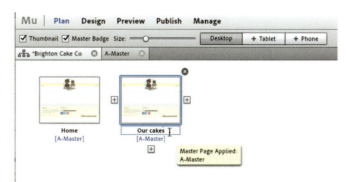

Designing the master page

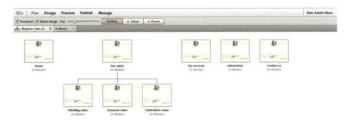

▶ Create three more pages to the right in the same way: Name them *Our Services*, *Information* and *Contact Us*. We also need three pages beneath the *Our Cakes* page. These will become the sub-menus for the product galleries. To do this, click the plus sign beneath the *Our Cakes* thumbnail. To create the rest, add two more to the right of that. This gives us the sub-page hierarchy. We'll name these pages *Wedding cakes, Seasonal cakes* and *Celebration cakes*.

Add a navigation bar

Go back to the **Design mode** so we can carry on editing the master page. Go to the docked panels. Select the **Widget Library panel**. We can see five main categories. Click the arrow next to the **Menus** item to open the list if it's not already visible. We have two options: **Horizontal** and **Vertical**.

Click and drag the **Horizontal** menu widget over to the page. Don't worry about the positioning for now, we just needed to place it on the design first.

Here's the default menu, it's already been populated with the current page structure. We also have an Options panel that gives us control over some of the design elements and options of the menu widget.

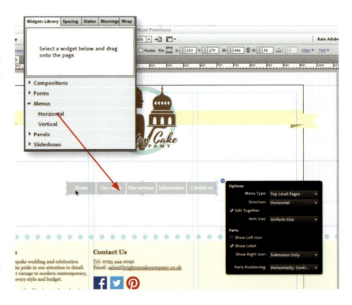

▶ Grab the **Selection tool**. Click and drag the menu up to the header graphic. Now use the left handle to stretch the menu across until it snaps to the edge of the content area. Do the same for the right edge. The width of the boxes changes to create equally sized items, leaving the text centered within them. This is controlled by the menu widget's Option panel. We'll look at this in more detail next. Use the top and bottom handles to stretch the height to match the ribbon.

The Menu Widget settings

Menu Type: this determines how the menu will display the pages of the site.

- **Top Level Pages** only displays the main pages of the site (at the top of the hierarchy).

- **All Pages** shows the top navigation level and all sub-level pages as drop-down items, depending on how they are arranged in the **Plan mode**.

- **Manual** lets us choose which links to pages or anchor tags to add. Page links are not automatically created and need to be added, along with the label text or image, for each item. New items are created by clicking the plus icons in the same way as adding pages in the **Plan mode**.

Direction: this can be set to **Horizontal** or **Vertical**. We can alternate between them at any time.

Edit Together: when this is enabled any change to a single item, text color for instance, will be applied to all elements of the menu uniformly. Disable this if you want to edit the items individually.

Item Size

- **Uniform Size** sets every item to the same width, regardless of the size of the label.

- **Uniform Spacing** sets the individual items to have varying widths, dependent on the label size.

Show Left Icon: this is disabled by default. When enabled a graphic element can be added to the menu items. This could be an image or have a fill color.

Show label: this, as the name suggests, determines if the item's text label appears or not. We would want to turn it off if we were using image-based menu items.

Show Right Icon: this is similar to the Show Left Icon item and has three settings

- **Off** – the icon is never displayed

- **On** – the icon is always displayed. The icon style is manually defined.

- **Submenus Only** – if the site has a hierarchy set up and the Menu Type is set to All Pages or Manual, the right-hand icon will be displayed. This is a downward-facing arrow by default but can be edited.

Parts Positioning controls how the items within each menu item are aligned.

- **Horizontally; Center Aligned** is the default setting. Text labels and icons are aligned in line along the horizontal center of the menu.

- **Horizontally; Top Aligned** sets the text labels and icons to be aligned in line to the top of the menu.

- **Vertically; Center Aligned** sets the text labels and icons to be aligned in line down the vertical center.

- **Vertically; Left Aligned** sets the text labels to be center aligned at the top of the menu item, icons are placed beneath the text label and left-aligned to the menu item.

2 Designing the master page

The navigation menu is in place but we need to make some changes. The website design doesn't include the home page as a standard menu item, instead, we'll add the link into the logo. We also need to change the appearance to something more suitable. All this is completely under our control, of course. We'll need to take a structured approach to this, however.

Style the menu

The objects in the menu object are arranged hierarchically, the first component in the tree being the menu itself. The next item to be selected appears as a tooltip as we hover the cursor over it. In this case, it's the menu item; click once to select it. The currently selected item is shown in the Selection Indicator in the far left of the **Control panel**.

It's worth making a point to remember this, as it's very easy to find yourself working on the wrong object!

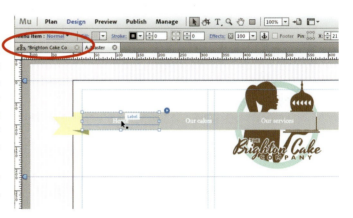

▸ The first thing we'll do is remove the background fill; we only want the text labels floating on the ribbon.

Click the **Fill** swatch in the **Control panel** to open the color picker. Click the top-left swatch (*None*). This removes the fill leaving us with just the text. It's not particularly clear at the moment, of course, as it's white on yellow.

▸ As these are buttons, we need to change the background for each of their states. Click where it says normal to the right of the object name in the **Control panel**. This gives us a list of the menu states. Click **Roll-over**. Set the color for this to *None* as we did in the previous step.

Repeat this for the remaining two states. It seems like we're only changing this one item, this is because it's the selected item; the rest will follow suit due to the **Edit Together** option being set in the widget's options. The changes will be apparent when the site is previewed.

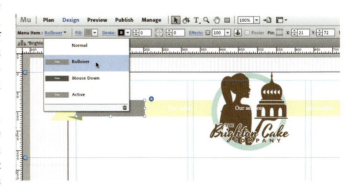

▶ With the background removed for the menu button states, we need to make the text clearer. We'll begin by changing the color so we can see the menu items properly. Click the first menu item a couple of times until the Label item is showing as selected in the Selection Indicator.

Open the **Text panel**. Click the color swatch to open the color picker. We'll use the *Chocolate Brown* preset for the normal state. As before, all the menu headings are changed in unison.

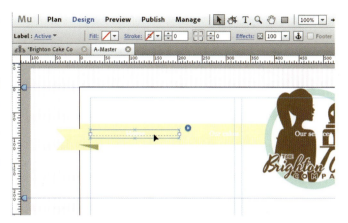

▶ Next, we'll change the remaining menu button states. Click the **Normal** state link in the **Control panel** to open the **States panel**. Select the **Rollover** item. Set the color to the *Mint Green* preset. It's a little faint now but will be more visible once we change the typeface and weight.

Leave the **Mouse Down** as it is but change the **Active** state to green as well; we need to show the visitor which page they are currently viewing.

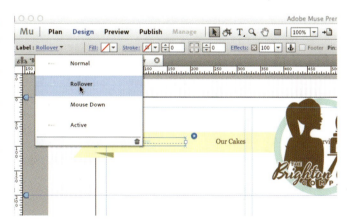

▶ Now for the typeface. Choose the **Normal** menu state again. Go back to the **Text panel**. Click the font dropdown menu. Click **Add Web Fonts** as we did previously. We want a sans serif font so we can click the filter option at the top of the window to narrow the choice. *Cabin* is a good clean font and has several weights available. Click **OK** to add it.

Go back to the font menu. Hover over the entry for *Cabin*. A sub-menu appears giving us the weights and styles. Choose **Bold**. Finally, set the size to **24px**. Check the other states to make sure they have followed suit.

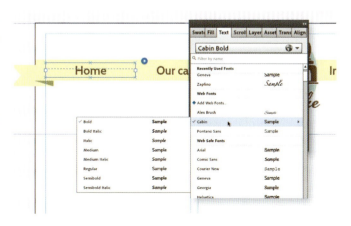

2 Designing the master page
Working around limitations

We need to change the layout of the menu to fit our design. Although the obvious solution would be to move the home page to the middle of the site plan to allow the menu items to fall either side, it brings to light a restriction in the way Muse handles the site files. The page on the far left of the site plan is always the page that loads first when the visitor comes to the site (the index page). If we move the home page, however, the index will default to *Our Cakes*, loading that first. There is currently no way to override this.

We have two options here: we can either change our design slightly or use a more complicated technique to allow us to still retain the current layout. In the interest of not over-complicating the process this early on, I decided to change the site design, moving the logo to the left of the site, with the menu items following. The technique for adjusting the layout whilst keeping the current design is explained in chapter 7.

Whilst we try to stick to the design we have agreed with the client, unlike print design, sometimes it's just not technically possible to achieve the exact layout we want. The menu issue here highlights this perfectly. Although it is possible to work around the problem, it's often better to take the easy option and prevent further complications later on down the line.

Menu display options

The first thing we need to do is remove the home page entry from the menu, as we'll be using the site logo as the link to navigate back. Go back to the **Plan mode** (**Cmd+M/Ctrl+M**). Right-click the *Home* page's thumbnail to open its contextual menu. Open the **Menu Options** sub-menu. Choose **Exclude From Menus**.

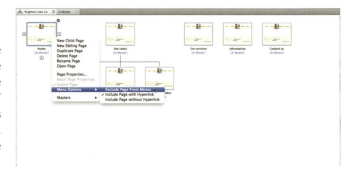

▶ Go back to the master page in the **Design mode** (**Cmd+I/Ctrl+I**). We can see that the menu no longer contains the home page. We'll have to make a few changes, of course, but it's going to be better in the long-term.

▶ First, we'll move the logo over to the left of the page. Grab the **Selection tool** (**V**). Click the logo image to make sure it's active. Hold down the Shift key to constrain the movement. Now drag the image across to the left so it aligns to the left-hand page guide.

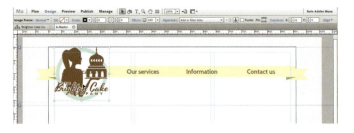

▶Let's change the size of the menu to fit alongside the logo. Click the menu widget to make it active. Drag the middle-left handle over to the right of the logo image. A smart guide will appear to show when the edges meet. The menu items are automatically spaced proportionately, so we don't need to make any further adjustments.

Image-based page link

With the menu set up we can make the logo into a link to the home page. Make sure it's the active object; it will display as *Image Frame* in the Selection Indicator. Go to the **Hyperlink** menu. Select *Home* from the list of internal links.

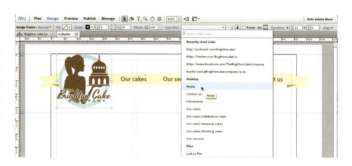

▶We need to have some kind of indication that the image is a live link. We could create a new version of the logo incorporating a rollover state, of course, but we can also apply effects directly in Muse.

Select the **Rollover** state in the **Control panel**. Click the Effects item to open its options panel. Click the third item tab to select the **Glow** settings. Enable Glow by clicking its checkbox. We'll use our *Mint Green* preset for the color.

Set the **Opacity** to **65** and the **Blur** value to **15**. This gives us a subtle halo around the logo that will display when the visitor hovers over it.

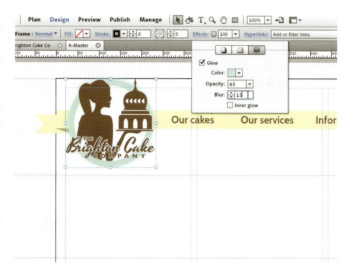

Open the **Hyperlink options panel**. Make sure that the option to open the link in a new window is unchecked; we don't want it branching off. We can also add a tooltip to further notify the visitor that the image is a link to the home page.

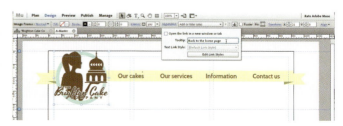

2 Designing the master page

Add sub-menus

Currently, we can only see the top level of menu items. *Our Cakes* has three sub-pages, so we'll need to enable them. Click any of the menu items to make it active. Click the blue arrow button to open the **Options panel**. Change the **Menu Type** to **All Pages**. Enable the **Show Label** option. Set it to **Sub-menus only**.

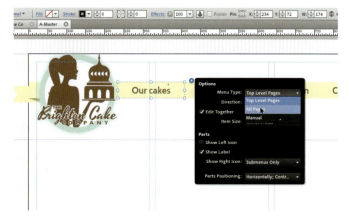

▶If the sub-menus aren't visible, we can open them by clicking on the *Our Cakes* menu item. On the live page, they will be displayed when we hover over the item.

The default sub-menu style doesn't match the style we've set up. We'll need to alter them individually.

▶We can give ourselves a helping hand with styling the menus by defining a paragraph style based on the main menu items.

Click to select one of the menu labels. Open the **Paragraph Styles panel**. Click the **New Paragraph Style** icon at the bottom. The style details dialog opens. We'll name this Main Menu.

▶To apply the style we need to select the menu item object of one of the sub-menus. Go over to the **Paragraph Styles panel**. Click the *Main Menu* style. All three menus now have the same typeface, size and color. Note that the style only affects the text, we'll need to adjust the menu frames separately.

▸ Although we have the correct typeface and color, the bold style of the main menu is a little too much for the sub-menus. Right-click the *Main Menu* paragraph style. Select **Duplicate Style**. Double-click the duplicate style's label. Change its name to *Sub Menu*.

▸ Go to the **Text panel**. Select *Cabin Regular* from the font menu. Set the size to **20**. This looks much better.

Notice how the new style label now has a plus sign next to it. This is warning us that the style has been altered. Right-click the style's label again. Select **Redefine style** to set the changes.

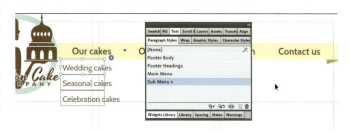

▸ We need to change the width of the sub-menu items. Click to select one of the sub-menu items. Click and drag the right-middle handle out to **160**. This gives us plenty of space for the page names to sit centered in their frames.

▸ We also need to change the background color. This will be the same as the main menu's background. Click one of the menu items to make sure it's still active. Open the Fill color picker. Use the **Sample Color tool** to sample the menu color. Create a preset named *Warm Yellow*

▸ The sub-menu states need to be altered as they are still set to the default values. Start by setting the Fill to *Warm Yellow* for the three remaining states. Now change the text color for the Rollover and Mouse Down states to *Mint Green*. The Active state should remain as *Chocolate Brown*.

2 Designing the master page

▶Currently, the sub-menus have a 1 pixel black stroke applied. This works well as a divider but is too bold for our site. Select the Normal state. Open the **Stroke options panel**. Click the chain icon to unlink the Stroke values. This allows us to alter them individually. Set the top value to **4 pixels**; change the rest to **0**. Go to the Stroke color picker. Set the color to white. Repeat this for the remaining states.

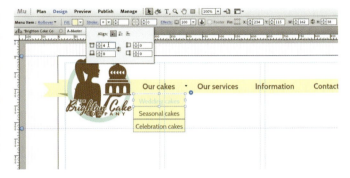

▶We only need to use the sub-menus for the cakes pages so we'll tell Muse not to use the main entry as a link.

Go to the **Plan mode** (**Cmd+M/Ctrl+M**). Right-click the thumbnail for *Our Cakes*. Go to the **Menu Options** sub-menu. Unlike the *Home* item, which we removed completely, we still want the item visible, so select **Include Page without Hyperlink**.

▶We've almost finished designing the master page. There are a few things to do before we start to create the site's page content.

Switch back to the Master in **Design mode** (**Cmd+I/Ctrl+I**). First we'll remove the fill and stroke from the page content area. Grab the **Selection tool** (**V**). Click anywhere inside the white area. Page will be displayed as the current item in the Selection Indicator. Go to the Fill color picker. Select the **No Fill** option. Now set the Stroke to **0**.

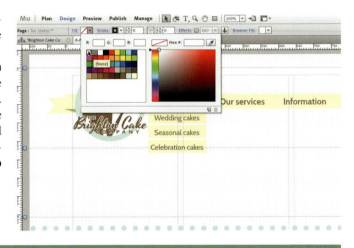

Protect the design layout

It's easy to accidentally move an object on the page without realising and if we're working on a live template, this could disrupt the whole site. We can prevent this from happening by locking the design's objects in place. This can be done on an individual basis, when we are happy with their position, by first selecting the object you want to lock then going to the Object menu and choosing Lock (**Cmd+L/Ctrl+L**). We can also lock every object at the same time by going to Edit > Select All (**Cmd+A/Ctrl+A**), then using the lock command.

The completed master page

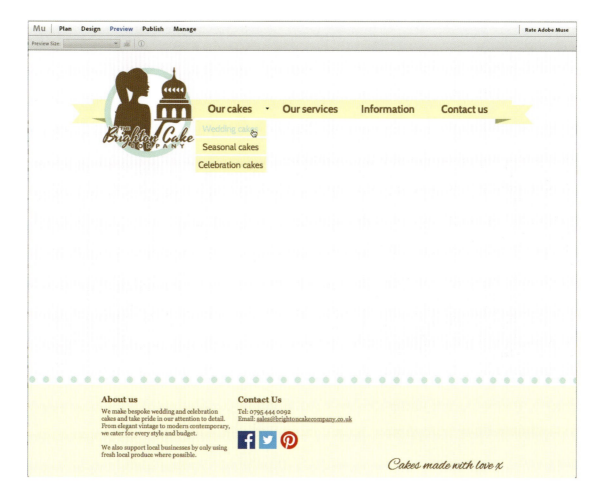

Here's the finished master page in Preview mode (Cmd+P/Ctrl+P). It's always a good idea to view your pages in preview every now and again, rather than relying on how it's seen in Design mode, as any mistakes in the design or setup will be easier to spot. We're now ready to begin creating the site content.

3 Creating the site content

With the master page complete, we can set about designing the site content based around it. Muse has some great built-in features for creating feature rich, interactive content. We'll be making good use of them in the following chapter.

3 Creating the site content
The home page

We'll start by setting up the home page. This is going to act as both a product showcase and a source of news about the company. We'll be using the built-in widgets to create a rotating display to draw visitors in, providing a direct link to the individual product galleries. We'll also create a section for upcoming events, news and a live feed from the company's Twitter account.

Build a slide presentation

The first element we'll create is the rotating product slide presentation using one of the built-in widgets. Rather than the preset slideshows, we'll use a Composition widget. This allows us to combine images, text and active elements on the slides.

Go to the **Widget Library panel**. Open up the Compositions list. We have several presets to choose from. We'll be working from scratch so choose the Blank. Click and drag it over onto the page. Don't worry about the exact positioning, we can alter that next.

▶ The widget's panel automatically expands out to a default size. Notice how the footer also drops down to accommodate it.

The basic Composition widget comprises two sections: the main area, referred to as the target, where the slide content is placed, and the three triggers below; these allow the visitor to select the targets manually, even if they are set to automatically cycle. The plus sign next to the last trigger can be clicked to add a new target and trigger. Coincidentally, the widget has three targets by default, which is also the number of categories in the cake company's product range, so we don't need to make any changes as yet.

The widget options panel also opens up to show the controls we have over the widget's behaviour; we'll look at them in more detail on the next page.

The Composition widget settings

The first setting is **Position**. This has three options and determines how the objects will be displayed:

- **Stacked** is the default setting of the basic preset. All targets are placed on top of each other and displayed according to the transition setting.

- **Scattered** allows the targets to be placed independently of each other on the page. This is the mode used by the Tooltip preset.

- **Lightbox** hides the targets initially and displays them on a semi-opaque overlay when the trigger is activated.

Show target determines how the targets will be activated. This has two options: On Click and On Rollover. The latter is not available in Lightbox mode.

Hide Target sets the display behavior of the target areas, enabling you to show or hide the content. Again, these are not available in Lightbox mode. This setting has four options:

- **None** keeps the activated target visible.

- **On Click** hides the target when the trigger is clicked.

- **On Rollout** hides the target as soon as the cursor leaves the trigger. Again, this is used with the Tooltip preset.

- **On Rollout of Trigger and Target** is similar to Rollout except the target also remains visible if the cursor is over it. This is used for creating pop-ups that have their own interactive items, such as buttons.

Transition controls how the target content will be displayed, replaced and hidden. This has three modes:

- **Fading** causes the content to fade in and out between the target content.

- **Horizontal** sets the content to slide in from the left or right, depending the whether the next slide is before or after the current target.

- **Vertical** sets the content slides in from the top or bottom of the target area.

Transition Speed controls the rate at which the targets are displayed. The arrows increase or decrease the amount in half-second increments or we can type in an arbitrary amount.

When **Auto Play** is enabled the targets will automatically cycle round when the page is loaded. The time delay between slides can be set in half-second intervals or entered manually. Ordinarily, when a composition is set to auto play the slides will be displayed in the order in which they were set up. We can randomize the order by checking the **Shuffle** option.

Hide All Initially prevents the targets from showing when the page is loaded, leaving only the triggers visible. This is mainly used for pop-up items such as tooltips but can be enabled for any of the Composition styles.

3 Creating the site content

Enable Swipe can be activated to allow the target content to be controlled by swiping on a touch-screen device such as the iOS and Android tablets and phones. It's an idea to leave this enabled in case visitors are viewing the desktop version on a mobile device.

By default, the target content is the top-most object in the composition object; moving the target over the triggers will hide them beneath. **Triggers on Top** forces the triggers to sit above the target content. This lets us have thumbnails and buttons that display above the target area if the design demands it.

The next section is **Parts**. Here we have the option to show the navigation (previous and next) and close buttons. As with the other widget components, these can be placed anywhere on the page.

The final section is **Editing**. These options are solely used during the creation process:

- **Show lightbox parts while editing** toggles the display of the target areas, enabling us to edit the content and also see the design layout without needing to switch between the Design and Preview modes each time.

- **Show all in Design Mode** shows every component of the composition without the need to click their targets. This is used primarily when creating pop-ups and other incidental items to aid in creating the layout.

▶ Let's begin creating our product display. Grab the **Selection tool**. Make sure that the overall Composition is the active object. Click and drag it over so the top-left corner aligns to the left page margin and the Header guide.

At this stage we can't increase the size of the composition as it takes its dimensions from the largest target object.

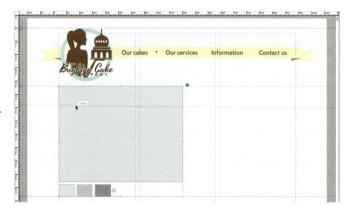

▶ Grab the **Selection tool**. Click to select the target object. Drag the right-middle handle over to the next column guide. This gives us a two-thirds span for the product slides. The height of the slides will be determined by the target content.

We'll leave the background fill for the time being as it helps with the positioning of the content.

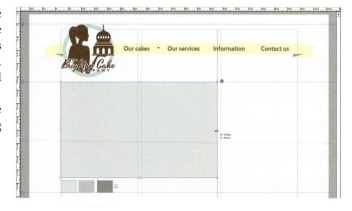

Add the slide content

Go to **File > Place** (**Cmd+D**/**Ctrl+D**). Navigate to the Assets folder. We can load the place gun with multiple images. For the first slide we need *wedding-cake.png*, *confetti.png* and *wedding-cakes-heading.png*. We can select them all by holding **Cmd**/**Ctrl** and clicking each in turn.

When we click **Open**, the cursor shows the thumbnail of the first image we selected – the confetti here – along with a number in brackets denoting the number of images that we loaded, 3 in our example.

▶Click once in the area to the right of the widget. The confetti image is placed onto the page. The cursor now shows the next image in the place gun. Click again to place this. Click once more to set down the final image.

At the time of writing it's not possible to place multiple images at their full size (using the single click method) directly onto a widget target.

▶The **Selection tool** is already active after placing the images. Click and drag the heading text image over to the widget. The boundary of the target turns blue to denote that we are adding items to it. Align the top-left corner of the bounding box to the left corner of the target.

3 Creating the site content

▶ Drag the cake image over to the widget, aligning the top-right corner to the right corner of the target. The height of the target expands to accommodate it. Lastly, drop in the confetti image.

▶ We need to change the stacking order of the image objects (sometimes referred to as the *Z order*) as the confetti is the front-most image and should be in the background.

Make sure the confetti is still the active object. Go to the **Object** menu. Select **Send to back**. This is relative to the target container of the Composition widget so it remains visible on the slide but is now behind the other items.

▶ Next we'll create the caption text. Grab the **Text** (**T**) tool. Click and drag out a text frame beneath the heading text. Make it fairly large, we'll adjust the dimensions once the caption is added. Type in the caption text as shown, or copy and paste from *captions.rtf* in the Assets folder.

▶Now let's style the text. Select the whole block of text. Go to the **Text panel**. Set the typeface to Georgia. Set the size to 20pt. Change the **Alignment** to **Centered**. Lastly, set the color to *Chocolate Brown*. Create a new paragraph style named *slide captions* so we can quickly apply it to the other slides.

▶Switch to the **Selection tool**. Use the handles on the text frame to fit it closer to the text. As we bring the bottom of the frame up, a dashed line appears just below the last line of text. This indicates the minimum height of the frame.

Although it's not relevant here, if we were creating a design with closely adjacent objects, we would need to pay attention to the height marker, as it could affect the layout when it's published.

▶We need to reposition the caption text. Click and drag inside the frame. We can use the Smart guides to make sure the caption is aligned horizontally with the heading and also vertically to keep it centered.

3 Creating the site content

▶ To add a little interaction to the slides, we'll create a link to the product galleries by means of a *Call to Action* button.

Go to **File > Place Photoshop Button** (**Cmd+B**/**Ctrl+B**). Open the *call to action.psd* file. The Photoshop import options dialog opens. The Normal and Rollover states are already set by the layer names. We just need to set the Mouse Down and Active states by choosing the layers from the drop-down menus. Click **OK** to load the place gun.

▶ Position the cursor over the target area, roughly in the position we want the button. Click once to place the button. Now click and drag the image into place; we can use the Smart guide to align with the center of the text. The Spacing guides can be used to set the vertical spacing equal to the spacing between the caption and the heading.

▶ We'll need to set the button as a link, of course. Open the hyperlink drop-down menu. Find the link *Our cakes: Wedding cakes*; sub-pages are prefixed with the parent page and a colon.

Open the **Hyperlink options panel**. Make sure that it's not set to open in a new window. Add some text for the tooltip. I've used *Jump to our gallery of wedding cakes*.

▶ That's the first slide completed. Currently, the triggers are hidden beneath the target area. Click the blue arrow to open the widget options panel. Enable the **Triggers on Top** option. Click the first trigger to make it the active object. Now hold **Shift** and click the other two. Drag the triggers down below the target area so we can work with them until the remaining slides are complete.

▶ Click the second trigger to activate its target. Repeat the steps we used to create the previous slide. This time use the images and text for the celebration cakes. Remember to set up the Call to Action button's link. Click the third trigger. Now add the *Seasonal cakes* slide content.

▶ Now that we have the three slides set up, we can remove the gray backgrounds. Make sure the target object is active by clicking an area of blank space. Open the **Fill Color panel**. Set the Fill to none. There's also a single pixel Stroke. Remove that by changing its value to **0**. Repeat this for each of the remaining slides.

3 Creating the site content

▸With the slide design for each target container complete, we can style the triggers. These will be used as both navigation and indicators of the currently displayed slide in the sequence. Rather than using images, we'll use the inbuilt styles.

Start by selecting the first trigger with the **Selection tool**. The wedding cake slide will be displayed.

▸Begin by making the trigger square by dragging right edge in slightly. Select the Active state from the **Control panel** or the **States panel**. Open the **Fill Options panel**. Set the color to *Chocolate Brown*. This defines the style of the trigger that displays for the currently active slide.

▸We could leave the trigger square but that doesn't fit with the theme. Go to the **Control panel**. Change the Corner Radius value to 20. This changes our square to a circle.

Let's stop at this point and create a graphic style for the circle shape. That way we can quickly apply the style to all three triggers. Open the **Graphic Styles panel**. Click the **New Style** icon. Double-click the style's label to open its properties. Change the name to *Trigger Active*. Click **OK** to apply.

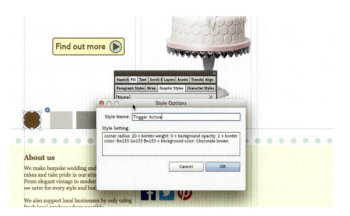

▶Select the trigger's Normal state. Click the *Trigger Active* style we just created; the colored circle style is applied. We don't want to change the original style. Right-click the style label. Select **Duplicate Style**. Rename this *Trigger Normal*.

Go to the **Fill panel**. Change the color to the *Mint Green* preset. The plus appears to tell us the style has been changed. Click the **Redefine Style** icon or right-click the style's label and select **Redefine Style** from the menu.

▶Now we'll style the Rollover state. Select it in the **States panel**. Apply the *Normal* style to give it the default look. Duplicate the style and rename as we did before; this time we'll call it *Trigger Rollover*.

We'll add a stroke to the circle that will appear as we hover over the trigger. Set the Stroke value to **4**. Set the Stroke color to *Chocolate Brown*. Redefine the style to preserve it. Finally, set the Mouse Down state to the same style by clicking off it and reselecting it.

▶Select the second trigger object. Change it to a square. Go through each state setting them to the associated style presets. Do the same for the third trigger.

The circles are a bit too big. Select the first trigger. Hold **Shift**. Now select the other two. We can now scale all three at once by clicking and dragging the bottom-right handle. A size of **30** is OK. While we have the triggers selected, we can move them into position. Here, I've placed them at the center of the slide, just below the target area.

3 Creating the site content

Set the Autoplay

With all the elements in place, we can set up the autoplay options for the Composition widget. Open the **options panel** by clicking the blue arrow; it's a good idea to select the main composition or target first, as that gives the panel more space.

Start by changing the Transition to Horizontal. This makes the slides look more dynamic as they change. Leave the transition speed at its default of 0.5 seconds. Enable Autoplay. We can leave the rest of the settings as they are.

Test the presentation

Now's a good time to test the slides. Switch to **Preview** mode (**Cmd+P**/**Ctrl+P**). All being well, the page should load and the slides should start to rotate; they shift to the left when autoplaying.

As the slides change, the triggers also move, alternating between the active and normal states. If we hover the cursor over the trigger, we see the stroke we applied to the Rollover state. Clicking any of the triggers will stop the autoplay and go directly to the associated slide. The chosen target will shift in from the left if it's before the currently active target, or from the right if it comes after in the sequence.

Add the information panels

To complete the home page, we'll add the 3 information panels to the right of the slides. These will contain static text as well as the company's latest Twitter tweet. We'll begin by creating and styling the containers.

Grab the **Rectangle tool (M).** Position the cursor at the intersection of the **Header guide** and the third column margin. Click and drag the box across to the right page margin and down to a height of **176** pixels.

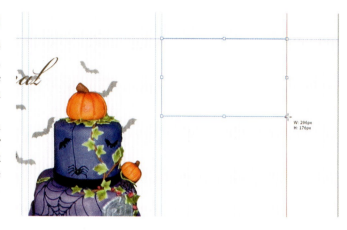

▶ Go to the **Fill panel**. Choose *Mint Green* for the Fill color. We don't want the containers to be too obtrusive so we'll lower the **Opacity** to **20**. This defines the space without overpowering the design.

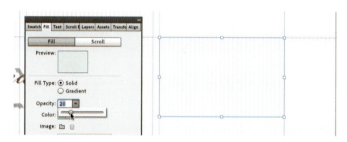

▶ We'll round off the corners to keep with the design theme. Change the **Corner Radius** to **10**. There's already a 1 pixel stroke, which looks good. All we need to do is change the Stroke color. Set this to *Chocolate Brown*.

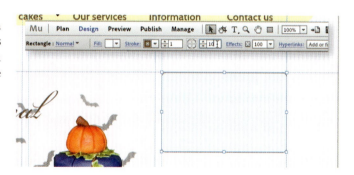

▶ It's likely that we'll use a similar box style elsewhere on the site, so before we continue, we'll create a new graphic style for the container. Go to the **Graphic Styles panel**. Click the **New Style** icon. Double-click the style label. We'll name this *Container*. Click **OK**.

Creating the site content

▶ Although we created a style for the boxes, we can quickly add the next two by copying the original. Grab the **Selection tool**. Hold down the **Opt/Alt** key. Now click and drag on the rectangle to make a copy. Repeat this for the third box. Make sure the boxes are aligned to the left column margin. Don't worry about the spacing for the moment.

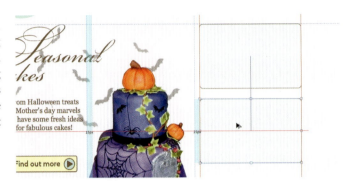

▶ We'll set the bottom of the last box to be parallel with the bottom of the slide triggers. Click and drag the rectangle vertically until the thicker blue guide appears to show that the two objects are aligned; we can hold the **Shift** key down as we move it to constrain the movement.

▶ Now we can adjust the spacing between the boxes. Ensure the bottom box is still selected. Hold the **Shift** key. Now click the two other boxes to add them to the selection. Access the **Align** settings in the **Control panel** or the **Align panel**. We'll use the **Distribute Vertical Centers** option here – the second to last icon in the **Distribute Objects** section – to set the vertical spacing equally.

Since we know this is where the boxes will remain, we can use this opportunity to lock them to the page (**Cmd+L/Ctrl+L**). This will prevent any accidental movement when we start adding the content.

Check your locked objects

(!) When copying and pasting objects, it's important to ensure that none of the items are locked, as they will not be included in the selection. Unfortunately, it's not possible to unlock items individually, it must be done at page level. The command for this is under the Object menu: **Unlock All on Page (Opt+Cmd+L/Alt+Ctrl+L)**. To avoid going through the process of locking the items again, if we undo (**Cmd+Z/Ctrl+Z**) the Unlock All command immediately after copying the objects to the clipboard, the objects will return to their previous state and the copied data will still be retained.

▶ The first box will contain the latest updates from the company. We'll begin by creating a heading. Grab the **Text tool**. Draw out a frame starting slightly offset from the edge of the box, across to the opposite side, leaving the same amount of space on the right. Type the heading, *What's new?* Select the text. We can use the *Footer Headings* style preset for this. Once added, we can lock it into place as we did with the box.

▶ Next, we'll add some content. Go to **File > Place** or press **Cmd+D**/**Ctrl+D**. Open *hitched award.jpg*. We don't need the full size image. Click and drag out the frame to 50%; a tooltip indicates the current percentage. Use the Smart guides to position the image so its top-left corner meets intersection of the base and left edge of the header.

▶ The content for the box is in the file *News. rtf.* Select and copy the text (excluding the URL). Press **Cmd+V**/**Ctrl+V** to paste it. Muse automatically creates a new text frame containing the text. It's just visible in front of the cake image here.

▶ Click and drag the text over to the box. Use the Smart guide to align the top of the frame to the top of the image. Leave a small margin between the text and the image. The text frame is too wide, so drag the right edge in until it aligns with the right edge of the header object.

Watch what you're pasting!

Text and rectangle frames are set to automatically expand vertically when the content within is too large. Occasionally, this can cause the rest of the page elements to be pushed down permanently, even if the objects are locked. Although this can be undone, it's always better to paste text elsewhere on the page first so we can edit it to size and then move it into position.

3 Creating the site content

▶ We're almost finished with the first box. Press **Return/Enter** to add a carriage return and drop the last line down to separate it from the previous paragraph. Select the whole block of text. Go to the **Paragraph Styles panel**. Apply the *Footer Body* preset.

▶ Now select the word *here*. Go back to the text file. Select and copy the URL. We can now paste it in to the Hyperlink menu to create a link to the page.

▶ We need to change the style of the link. We could use the preset we created for the footer email but we want to keep the visited attribute different to show when the link has been used previously.

Open the **Content** tab of the Site Properties dialog by clicking the **Edit Link Styles** button in the **Hyperlinks panel**. Select the *Footer Email* link style. Click the **New Link Style** icon to create a duplicate of the style. Double-click its label to edit the name. Name it *Box Link*.

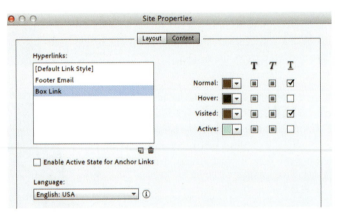

▶ The only color we need to alter is the Visited link state. Choose the *Mint Green* preset to set the base color.

Now drag the indicator down in the color spectrum to make it a darker shade. Click **OK** to set the style.

▶ Go back to the **Hyperlink panel**. Check the option to open the link in a new window. Set the Text Link Style to *Box Link*. Finally, add the tooltip. Here I've used *Go to the Hitched award site*.

▶The next box is for upcoming events. This is almost the same setup as the news box. Create the Events heading. Now open *Events.rtf.* Copy and paste the text for the two events into Muse and format it with the *Footer Body* style, making the date entries bold; I've created the two as separate elements to make it easier to change for the client. As before, apply the URL and email links separately.

Embedding HTML code

The final box is a little different. Here we'll be displaying the latest tweet from the company's Twitter feed. This requires us to create embedded HTML code that draws the information into the page. To streamline the process here, I've created a text file with the necessary code; you can create your own embed code by visiting *www.twitter.com/settings/widgets*.

As with the previous boxes, we'll begin by creating the heading: *Latest from Twitter*. Open the file *Twitter code.rtf*. Select and copy the entire contents. Come back into Muse. Go to the **Object** menu. Select **Insert HTML**. Paste the code into the HTML window. Click **OK** to apply.

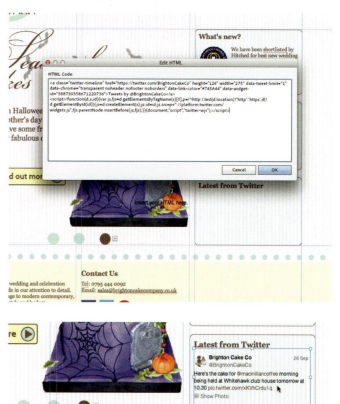

▶A new frame has been created on the page. After a short time, when it connects to Twitter to generate the display, we'll see the most recent tweet appear. All we need to do now is use the **Selection tool** to reposition the object inside the box.

3 Creating the site content
The gallery pages

The next set of pages we'll be creating is the product gallery. We'll be using another of the widgets included with Muse here, this time it's the Slideshow widget. This is similar to the Composition widget we used for the home page but is specifically designed for displaying photos.

Add the page description

Go back to the **Plan mode**. Double-click the *Wedding cakes* page thumbnail to open the page in **Design mode**. We'll start with the page header and caption.

Open the file *Gallery page text.rtf*. Select and copy the wedding cake section of the text. Paste it into Muse to create a new text frame. Use the **Selection tool** to position it against the left margin of the first column and the Header guide. Resize the frame so it spans the column width.

▶ Select the *Wedding cakes* heading. Go to the **Paragraph Styles panel**. Click the *Footer Headings* style to apply it to the text. We'll increase the size a little as it needs to be more prominent. Open the **Text panel**. Set the size to **24**.

As we'll be using this again, we'll create a new paragraph style. Duplicate the current style. Rename it to *Page caption header*.

▶ Now for the caption body. Select the text in the two paragraphs. Apply the *Footer Body* preset. As this is a larger block of text, we'll set the **Alignment** to **Justified**. Click the **Align Justify** icon in the **Text panel**.

Create a new style preset named *Page caption body*. Now highlight the company name on the first line. Set its style to **Italic**. The plus sign appears next to the style but we'll ignore it, as we need to retain the changes we've made.

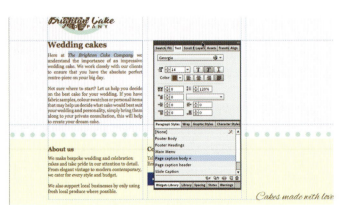

Build the slideshow

The **Slideshow widget** has little in the way of styling options, so we'll create a background for both the thumbnails and the hero (main) image.

Grab the **Rectangle tool**. Draw out a frame to the right of the caption we just created, leaving a gap roughly twice the width of the column margin, over to the right edge of the page. Align it to the Header guide. As yet we don't know exactly how high the frame needs to be so bring it down to around double the height of the caption.

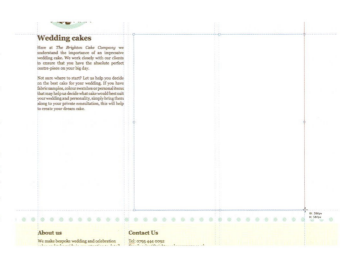

▶ We can use the same style for the frame background as we did for the boxes on the home page. Go over to the **Graphic Styles panel**. Click the *Container* style. This gives us the low-opacity green background with rounded corners.

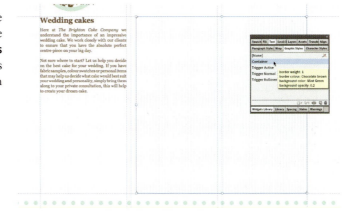

▶ Create another rectangle beneath the caption, leaving a reasonable amount of space below the text. Align the bottom of the frame with the main frame. Apply the *Container* style to this frame as well. This will be the background area for the block of thumbnail images.

3 Creating the site content

The slideshow settings

Now to add the Slideshow widget itself. Go to the **Widget Library**. Open the *Slideshow* folder. Click and drag the Basic preset over to the page.

By default there's a sample image with caption, navigation and counter. The options panel is very similar to that of the Composition widget, so I'll skip the full breakdown of its features and deal only with the settings specific to the slideshow.

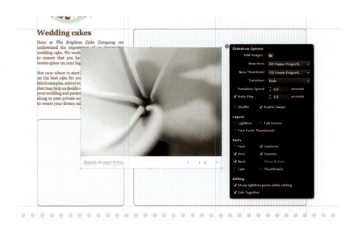

▶ We'll define the height of the hero image and its frame by the size of the thumbnail panel. We'll need to add some images, of course. Before we import them, we'll make some changes to the settings.

First, we'll set the **New Hero** option to **Fit Content Proportionally**. This ensures that the whole image will be visible to begin with. Next, turn off the **Captions** and the **Counter**. All we need is the navigation buttons. Finally, enable **Thumbnails**, as they're not currently visible.

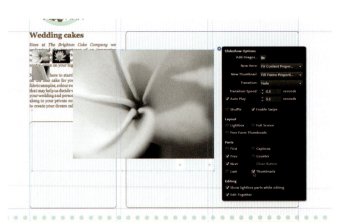

Import the images

▶ With the options set, we can add the first batch of images. There will be eight images per page. Click the **Add Images** icon. Browse to the *Wedding Cakes* in the *Assets* folder. Open the *Page 1* folder. Select all the images inside the folder. Click **Open**. Muse will begin importing the images. After a short time, we see them appear as thumbnails. These will automatically replace the sample images. If we add images at a later stage, they will be appended.

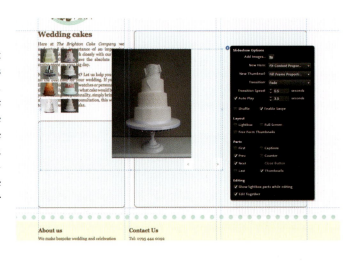

Position the thumbnails

Click on the thumbnails until the Thumbnail Container shows as the active object in the **Control panel**. Drag the container onto the panel we created. Leave a fairly generous border. Now drag out the right side of the container to the opposite side of the panel, leaving an equal border. This sets the boundary width for the thumbnails.

▶We want two columns of four thumbnails. Click the first thumbnail to make it active. Go over to the **Transform panel**. Set the **Width** to **120** and **Height** to **80**. As we do, the rest of the thumbnails change size to match.

Drag the bottom of the thumbnail container's frame up to meet the bottom of the thumbnails to remove the excess space that's pushing the footer down.

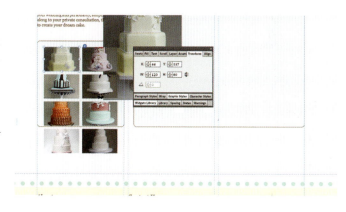

▶Now we have the height of the thumbnail frame, we can alter the backgrounds to match. Select the rectangle behind the thumbnails. Drag it down to make an equal border at the bottom.

Do the same with the hero image frame, aligning it with the thumbnail background.

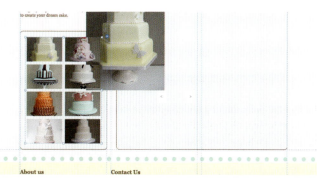

Order! Order!

The images are imported into the slideshow in alphabetical order, based on their file names. This isn't always how we want them to be displayed, of course. If we were the completely organized types, we could make sure the names are set to begin with, perhaps by numbering them. That's far too laborious, so Muse allows us to reorder them on-the-fly. All we have to do is select one of the thumbnail objects within the container and drag it to its preferred location. The new position is marked with a vertical blue bar. When we drop it in, the rest of the thumbnails are shuffled around it.

3 Creating the site content

Set the hero image size

With the thumbnails in place we can concentrate on the hero image. Click the current full size image until the hero Image is the active object. We'll start by lining up the bottom of the image with the base of the thumbnails to give us the border size to work from. Drag the frame to the top-right corner, leaving the same border around the whole frame. We're setting the dimensions of the image frame here, not the image size, as this will cause the images to display with a uniform size as much as possible.

▶ Although we set the hero image to fit the frame proportionately, resizing the frame has not altered the photo. Go to the **Object** menu. Select **Fitting > Fit Content Proportionately**. The photo's dimensions change to make the best use of the frame; in this case, it's filled the vertical space.

▶ We'll need to do this for the rest of the photos in the set, of course. Click each of the thumbnails in turn to make the image active. Click the hero image to make sure it's the active element before using the **Fit** command again, otherwise it will apply it to the thumbnail instead.

▶ The next task is to style and position the navigation objects. We'll be using simple text items here. Select the *Next* object with the **Selection tool**. Stretch it out as we're going to need space to add the word *Next* behind the chevron.

Now double-click inside to activate the text label. Type the text in. Now do the same for the *Previous* object, adding the word *Previous* in front of the chevron. Select the whole text. Change the text color to *Chocolate Brown*. Both objects use this color.

▶ We don't want the background color. Grab the **Selection tool** again. Select the *Previous* button. Go to the **Fill panel**. Set the Fill to *None*. Again, both objects change together.

▶ Move the *Next* item just below the bottom of the outer hero frame so its chevron aligns with the column guide. Now position the *Previous* item next to it, leaving a little space in between the two.

Overcome the limited button styling

Unlike the Composition widget's trigger elements, we have limited control over the styling of the slideshow's directional buttons. By default they're text-based chevrons, we can change them to any text character but that's unlikely to be any prettier. There are a couple of workarounds, however; we can add a graphic element (see page 80) or download and install the *Font Awesome* library from the Muse Exchange. Details on how to do this can be found here: *http://muse.adobe.com/exchange-library/font-awesome*.

3 Creating the site content

Create a breadcrumb trail

Since we are having three pages of wedding cakes, we'll need a way of navigating between them. We could have another set of sub-menus hanging off the main navigation but that could look untidy. Instead, we'll use another menu widget to create a breadcrumb trail navigation.

Go to the **Widgets Library**. Drag a horizontal menu over to the page. Place it in the area under the thumbnails; we'll fine-tune the position later.

▶By default the menu is set to include the top-level pages. We don't want this, of course. Set the **Menu Type** to **Manual** in the **Options panel**. This gives us full control over the menu content. We're left with a single item.

Drill down to select the text item of the menu. Change it to *Page 1*. Select the whole text. Now set the color to *Chocolate Brown*.

▶The menu will be text only so we need to remove the background. Use the **Selection tool** to make the menu item active. Make sure the Normal state is selected. Go to the **Fill panel**. Set the **Fill** to *None*.

Switch to the Rollover state. Remove the background as before. Go to the **Text panel**. Set the color to *Mint Green*. Do the same for the Mouse Down state.

We need to indicate which page we're on. Switch to the Active state. Remove the background. Keep the brown text color but make the text bold.

▶ We need to have three menu items. Click the plus icon to the right of the menu frame to create a new item. Select the second item. Click the plus icon again to create a third menu item.

▶ We want the menu label text to be aligned to the left edge of the thumbnail box. We could reposition the menu as it is, with the edge of its frame overhanging the content area but there's a tidier way.

Click to select the Label item of one of the menu items. Go to the **Text panel**. Select the **Align Left** icon. All three items shift over to the left. We can now position the menu to butt against the column guide.

▶ The last part of the menu styling is to alter the spacing. Drag the right edge of the frame over to the left. We want a small gap in between the items. A width of around **180px** gives us good spacing.

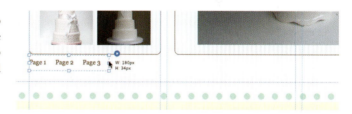

▶ Although we have the three menu items, they are not yet linked to anything. Use the **Selection tool** to make the Page 1 menu item active. Go to the **Hyperlink** menu. Choose the internal link *Our Cakes: Wedding cakes*. Go to the Hyperlink Options. Set the tooltip to *Wedding cakes: Page 1*.

When we click away from the menu, *Page 1* is emboldened to show that it's the current page. We'll need to create the other two pages to be able to link to them, of course.

3 Creating the site content

▶ We can use the current gallery page as a template for the rest, as very little is going to differ in the layout. Go back to the **Plan mode**. Right-click the *Wedding cakes* page thumbnail. Select **Duplicate**. A copy of the page is created to the right. Rename it *Wedding cakes 2*.

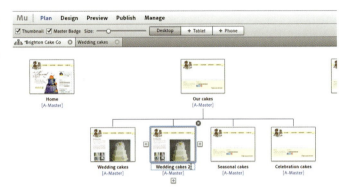

Alter the page hierarchy

The new page is in the wrong part of the site hierarchy. Click and drag it over the label of the original gallery page. The area turns blue. Release the mouse and the thumbnail will move to the position below the first page. This is tidier and will set up the site-map properly.

▶ We need another duplicate. There's a quicker way to do this. Click the second page's thumbnail. Now hold down **Opt/Alt**. Drag the thumbnail to the right of the second page's label. The blue area appears again. Release the thumbnail. Another copy is created next to it. Rename this page *Wedding cakes 3*.

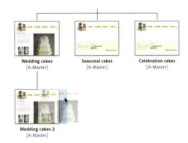

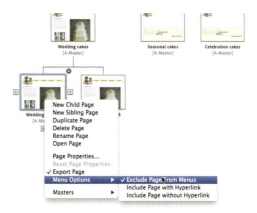

▶ Currently, the two new pages will show up as sub-menus to the main *Wedding cakes* menu item. We don't want this to happen, as we have set up our separate menu. Right click *Wedding cakes 2*'s thumbnail. Select **Exclude Page From Menus** from the **Menu options**. Repeat this for *Wedding cakes 3*.

▶ Now we have the three gallery pages, we can finish up the page navigation menu.

Go back to the original gallery page. Select the *Page 2* menu item. Go to the Hyperlink menu. Select *Our Cakes: Wedding cakes: Wedding Cakes 2*. Set the tooltip to *Wedding cakes: Page 2*. Repeat this for page 3.

▶ We need to do this for the menus on pages 2 and 3 as well. Double-click each page in turn to open it in the **Design mode**. Page 1 of the menu is already set as it's copied from the original.

Set the links for pages 2 and 3 as before. Move on to page 3 and do the same. Muse will automatically assign the correct active states for each page.

3 Creating the site content

Replace slideshow content

▶ We have the additional pages but the content is just a copy of the original at the moment. There's currently no way of automatically replacing the images in the slideshow, so we'll have to do this in two stages.

Select the last thumbnail in the set (bottom-right) to make it active; new content is always added after the currently selected image. Open the **Options panel**. Click the folder to bring up the file dialog. Browse to the Page 2 folder. Select the eight images. Click **Open**. The new images will be added.

▶ The last thumbnail of the original set is still selected. Hold **Shift**. Now click each of the first thumbnails in turn to add them to the selection.

Once they're all selected, press the **Delete** or **Backspace** key. This removes the selected items, shifting the new set up to fill their place. As the new images were appended, there's no need to alter the thumbnails or the hero images as they take on the previous attributes.

▶ That's the second set of images in place. The only adjustment we need to make is to shrink the thumbnail container to its original height, as it was stretched to accommodate the additional thumbnails and has pushed the footer down. Click and drag the bottom of the frame up to the base of the thumbnails. The footer will return to its original position.

Go through the previous steps for the final page, adding the remaining images from the *page 3* folder.

Duplicate the widgets

As we already have pages defined for the other product galleries we'll use a different method to replicate the slideshows.

Go to one of the wedding cake pages. Grab the **Selection tool**. Position the cursor adjacent to the top-right corner of the hero frame. Click and drag down towards the area just below the thumbnail container. A blue box appears as we do; everything within the box will be selected. Stay to the right of the page menu, we don't need that selected as the other galleries are only going to be single pages.

Go to **Edit > Copy** (**Cmd+C/Ctrl+C**) to copy the selected objects to the clipboard.

▶Go back to **Plan mode**. Double-click the *Seasonal cakes* page thumbnail to open it in the **Design mode**.

Go to back to the **Edit** menu. Select **Paste in Place** (**Opt+Shift+Cmd+V/Alt+Shift+Ctrl+V**). This places all the objects in exactly the same position on the page they were copied from.

Open the *Gallery pages* text file again. Select and copy the *Seasonal cakes* section. Delete the existing text from the page caption. Replace it with the copied text. Now exchange the images for the files in the *Seasonal cakes* assets folder.

Repeat this process for the *Celebration cakes* page to complete gallery page content. Remember that we can reorder the image positions (see tip on page 65).

see tip on page 65

Adjusting the thumbnail images

The thumbnails are set to fill the frame proportionately. Since most of our images are portrait and the thumbnail containers are landscape, the images are clipped and are not always displayed at a good viewpoint. It is possible to adjust them manually, however. We can scale them to zoom in on the detail or reposition the content. The method for doing this is described over the page. To apply it to our slideshow thumbnails, we simply select each thumbnail in turn to adjust it.

3

Creating the site content
Our services page

The next page is *Our Services.* **As well as revisiting previous techniques and styles here, we'll be looking at some of the more powerful effects and tools available in Muse for working with images and text. We'll create a montage of images showing the detail of some of the cakes to add a highlight to the page. We can rotate the images on-the-fly, which gives us greater flexibility as we design the page in the Muse workspace.**

▶ We'll begin by setting the text. Open the file *Services text.rtf.* Select and copy the body text.

Come back to the page and paste it in. We'll use the same styles for the heading and body that we used for the gallery pages.

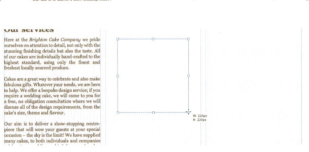

Create a frame template

We'll create a frame template to hold the images. Grab the **Rectangle tool** (**M**). Hold **Shift** to constrain the proportions to a square. Click and drag out a frame, around 220 pixels is a good size.

▶ Set the Stroke color to white. Set the size to **10**. The default position for a stroke is centered to the edge of the object. Go to the **Stroke options**. Set the **Position** to **Inside** by selecting the middle icon.

▶ Set the Fill color to something with a strong contrast. I've used dark green here. This is just so we have a better visual guide for aligning the image content. We can change it once the images have been added.

▶ The final part of the frame template is to add a small drop shadow. Go to the **Effects panel**. Select the **Drop Shadow** tab. Click the Shadow checkbox to enable to effect. We'll keep most of the default settings apart from the distance. Lower that to **2**. This gives us a subtle separation from the background.

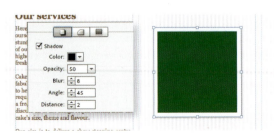

74

▶ That's the basic settings for the frame. Let's create a graphic style with these attributes. Go to the **Graphic Styles panel**. Click the **New Style** icon. Double-click the style label to open the properties dialog. We'll name it *Frame*.

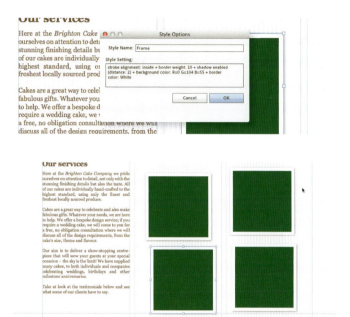

▶ Grab the **Selection tool**. Hold down **Opt/Alt**. Click and drag the frame to make a duplicate. Do this twice more. For now, we'll space them out to make it easier to add the images.

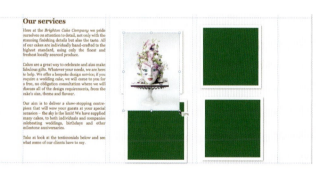

▶ We'll start adding the images. Go to **File > Place** (**Cmd+D**/**Ctrl+D**). Browse to the *Services Images* folder. Select the face cake image.

Click **Open** to load the place gun. Position the top-left corner over the top-left of the green fill of the first frame. Click and drag the corner of the image as you are placing it, until its width covers the frame's interior.

Using the Crop tool

Grab the **Crop tool** (**C**). Drag the bottom handle of the image up. As we do the image turns translucent so we can see the frame beneath.

Rather than scaling the image, however, we're trimming it down to the size of the frame. Bring it just inside the border. We can tell if it's gone too far as we'll start to see the green fill.

3 Creating the site content

We want to zoom in on the detail in these photos. Hover the cursor over the image, a circle appears in the center. Click once. The frame turns brown, showing us the full area of the image. Click and drag the bottom-right corner. Again, the image goes translucent as it expands.

If we hold down **Opt**/**Alt** as we drag, the image resizes from its center. The display by the cursor tells us the current percentage of the image's full size – around **42%** works well here. When we release the mouse, only the area within the frame is shown.

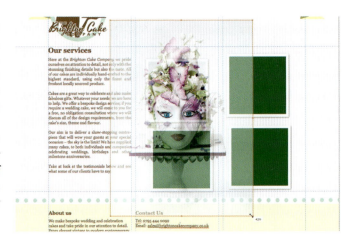

Once we've resized the image, we can click and drag inside the frame to position it. We can also press the **Arrow keys** on the keyboard to nudge it for more accuracy.

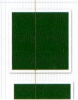

The last thing we'll do is group the photo and its frame. This will enable us to move and rotate it as a single object. Grab the **Selection tool**. Click away from the image frame to deselect it.

Now click inside the frame again to select the visible image frame. Hold **Shift** down. Click the border. We now have both selected. Go to **Object > Group** (**Cmd+G**/ **Ctrl+G**) to combine the objects.

Repeat the previous steps to add in the remaining images. Zoom in to highlight the particular details of each. Remember to group each pair of objects after creating them.

Rotating images

Now we can start putting the images into position. We'll start with the face cake. Use the **Selection tool** to select the group. Hover the cursor just outside of one of the frame's corners. The cursor will change to a circular arrow. When we click and drag, the image rotates clockwise if we drag down or counter-clockwise if we drag up.

▶Rotate and reposition the rest of the images. We can have them overlapping for the scattered effect. We can also change their stacking order here, moving the third image beneath the first. Either select the first image, then go to **Object > Bring to Front**, or select the third image and choose **Object > Send Backward**. We can also right-click the image and use the **Arrange** menu item.

▶The cropping and rotation is rendered live in the browser. This means that occasionally, we'll get slight misalignments. This could result in seeing the green background.

Use the **Selection tool** to select one of the rectangles. Change its Fill color to white. Now go to the **Graphic Styles panel**. Click the **Redefine Style** icon. All four image frames will now have white backgrounds, as they share the style. Any inaccuracies in the live version should now be invisible.

Effects on-the-fly

Many of the effects and transformations in the design are generated in real time, via the CSS code that Muse generates, when the page is opened in the browser. This includes more sophisticated actions such as glows, drop-shadows and image rotations. When we publish the page, cropped images will usually be adjusted to match the size of the crop. This means the file size will be smaller, taking up less space on the server, it will be much quicker to upload and the page will load faster. There is an exception, however; if the image is used elsewhere on the site, it will remain at its largest size and the cropping will be done by the browser.

3 Creating the site content

Create a page divider

Let's move on to the testimonials section mentioned in the caption body. We'll begin by creating a divider between the top and bottom sections of the page.

Grab the **Rectangle tool**. Position the cursor just below the bottom of the upper content but above the Footer guide. Draw out a frame of **860px** wide by **2px** high. Use the **Selection tool** and Smart guides to reposition it in the center of the page, leaving a reasonable amount of space from the bottom of the images and text.

▶ Set the Rectangle's Fill color to *Warm Yellow*. Set the Stroke value to **0**. Go to the **Effects options panel**. Select the **Bevel panel**. Check the Bevel option to enable it. The defaults are too much. Leave the **Opacity** at **75**. Set the **Blur** to **2**. Leave the **Angle** at **45**. Set the **Distance** to **2**. This gives us a subtle raised effect.

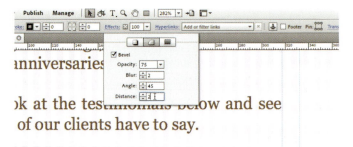

▶ Select the **Text tool**. Draw out a text frame, again it needs to be above the Footer guide. Add the text *What our customers are saying*. We'll use the *Footer Heading* paragraph style here. Drag the frame out to accommodate the text on a single line, if it's too large. Set the **Alignment** to **Center** so we can use the Smart guides to align it to the page.

Now click and drag the frame to the center of the page. We can use the Spacing guides to create the same amount of vertical spacing as we have between the horizontal rule and the upper content – the amount of space (in pixels) is temporarily displayed as you drag each element on the page.

▶ Go back to the *Services.rtf* file. Select and copy the first quote. Paste it onto the page. Position the edge of the frame against the left page margin. Leave an adequate margin below the heading.

▶ We'll use the *Footer Body* style as the basis for the quote style. Select it from the **Paragraph Styles panel**. The text is too small so increase the size to **16**. Click the **New Style** icon to create a new paragraph style. We'll call it *Testimonials*.

▶ Next, we'll set up the background style. Go to the **Graphic Styles panel**. Choose the *Container* style. We'll make the background completely opaque for the quotes. Go to the **Fill Options panel**. Increase the **Opacity** to **100**. Create a new graphic style named *Quotes container*.

▶ The frame is a little tight around the text. We can adjust this by adding space around the text. Go to the **Text panel**. Set the **Space Before** value to 6. Set the **Space After** to 6. Change the **Right Margin** to 8. This gives the text some breathing space. We'll need to update the style settings with the **Redefine Style** icon.

3 Creating the site content

▶ Grab the **Selection tool**. Drag the right edge of the text frame across to the right until the quote only spans two lines. This will be adequate for the majority of the quotes.

▶ The next part of the quote box is to have a speech balloon to the left of the text. Go to **File > Place** (**Cmd+D**/**Ctrl+D**). Open the *talk-bubble.png* file. Click once to drop it onto the page. The position isn't important.

Wrap text around an image

We want the text and the image to interact so the text fits to the edge of the balloon. If we were to drag the image onto the box, it would simply cover the text. If we were to set the balloon as the background fill it would appear beneath the text. Instead, we'll use the text-wrapping feature. To do this we must paste the image into the text frame. Go to **Edit > Cut**. This copies the image to the clipboard and removes it from the page.   Double-click the text frame to make it active. Position the text cursor at the beginning of the top line. Go to **Edit > Paste**. The balloon now pushes the text content aside.

▶ Switch back to the **Selection tool**. Drag the bottom-right corner of the balloon's frame to scale it down. Around **70%** is a good size. Go to the **Wrap panel**. Currently the **Wrap** is set to **Inline**; the image behaves like a piece of text. We want the whole caption to butt against it. Click the **Left Wrap** icon. The balloon is now positioned flush with the text. We'll need to adjust the width of the frame again but we have a couple of adjustments to make first.

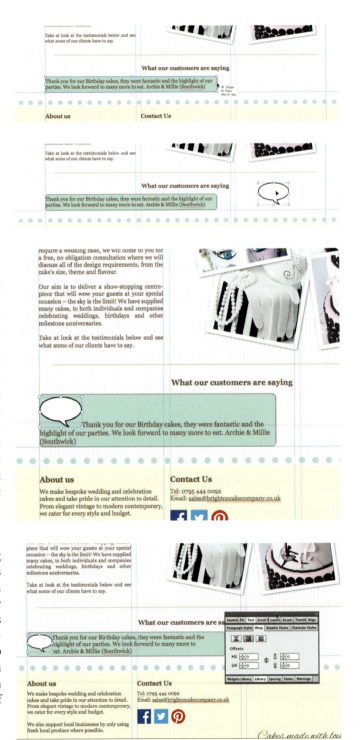

▶We need to add a margin between the balloon and the text. This is done by increasing the **Right Offset** setting. A value of **8** is good. We can also use negative values. This lets us offset the image outside of the frame for effect. Set the **Top Offset** to **-10**. Now set the **Left Offset** to **-8**. This sets the balloon to hang off of the left corner.

▶Drag out the right edge of the container to set the text to two lines again. We'll add a drop-shadow as we did with the photos. Go to the **Shadow** section of the **Effects panel**. Click to enable it. Change the **Distance** to **2**. Remember to update the style afterwards.

Create a library item

Up to now we've used custom styles to define the formatting and appearance of page elements. These only let us describe the attributes of a single element at a time. We could use individual styles to define the component parts of our quote object but we would still have to recreate them piece by piece. There's a better way. Muse has a feature called the Library, which provides the ultimate control over saving and applying styles. We can add complex, reusable elements that we simply drag onto the page, a little like widgets.

Right-click the quote container. Select **Add to Library** from the menu. A folder is created containing the new item.

▶Double-click the library item. Name it *Quote Container*. Library items are stored globally so we could use the item in any site we create. This can quickly become cluttered. Name the newly created folder *Brighton Cake Co* so we know where to come looking for a particular object.

3 Creating the site content

Reusing a library item

When we click the new item we created, we get a thumbnail view of it in the window above. To add a new instance to the page we simple drag the thumbnail or the item name onto the page content. A preview with plus sign appears under the cursor. Release the mouse to drop the new item.

▶ Move the new quote object into position below the original. We'll place this one aligned to the right edge of the page content. The original text was stored when we created the library item. Double-click the text to make it active. Select the entire block of text.

Go back to the text file. Select and copy the next quote. Paste it into the container to replace the old text. Use the **Selection tool** to pull the left edge in a little to fix the widowed text at the end of the sentence.

▶ Add the remaining quotes in the same way, alternating from left to right down the page. Stretch or contract the containers to suit the text. I've also increased the spacing between the containers to **60px** to avoid them looking too cluttered.

As a final touch, we can select the people's names and set the style to *Italics*. This separates them from the rest of the text.

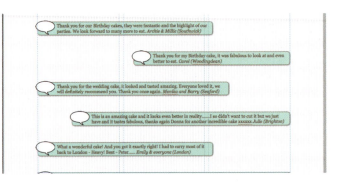

Your site vs the rest of the world

Often when we create page elements in Muse, they can appear slightly differently when previewed, either in Muse or a browser. For instance, when I stretched out the containers, the text was set to two lines and looked great. When I previewed the page, however, the text in some had been pushed down to 3 lines. This is not a shortcoming of Muse, the engineers have done a fine job with cross-platform coding. Anything we publish to the Internet is at the mercy of the visitor's PC setup, as they may have increased or decreased the text size, which overrides the design formatting. It's well worth previewing often to make sure everything works. There's a great online resource called *BrowserShots (http://browsershots.org)* that renders any given page in almost every available browser and platform.

The Information page

The *Information* page is going to be a little different in style to the previous pages. The focus will be on a single information panel in the center, rather than the separate text and image combination we've been using so far. We'll be using another widget available in Muse, called the Accordion panel. This is a series of individual sections that collapse when the next is displayed. Accordion panels encapsulate a great deal of visual content into a small area of screen real estate.

▶ We'll start with the page heading. Grab the **Text tool**. Draw out a reasonably wide text frame, aligned to the Header guide. Use the **Selection tool** to drag the frame so it aligns to the center of the first page content column; a vertical red guide appears when we hit the center.

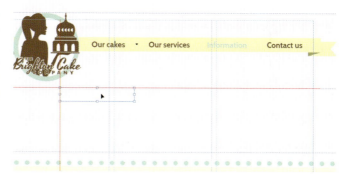

▶ Go back to the **Text tool** if you swapped to the **Selection tool**. Click inside the frame. Type in *Information*. Go over to the **Paragraph Styles panel**. Apply the *Page Heading* style. Tidy the frame by dragging the bottom handle up until we see the minimum size marker.

Add an Accordion widget

Go to the **Widget Library**. Click the Panel section to expand it and see the list of Panel widgets. Drag the Accordion widget over to the page. Leave a space below the heading around the same height as the text frame. Align the left edge of the widget to the left column center. Now drag the right side of the widget frame over to the center of the right column.

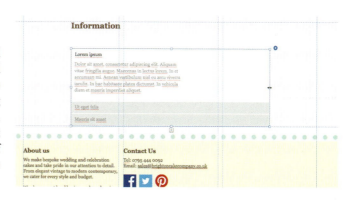

3 Creating the site content

Style the accordion panels

The default accordion has three sections, filled with *Lorem Ipsum* placeholder text. We'll start by styling the headings. These are similar to the labels inside menu items, and they also have four states. Use the **Selection tool** to select the first label. Active is the state for the currently visible panel.

▶ Apply the *Footer Heading* style. We need to alter the style slightly, as the Space After setting is increasing the height of the label. Set it to 0. Now drag the bottom of the label frame up as far as it will let you.

Duplicate the style. Name it *Label Active*. Click the **Redefine Style** icon to keep the new settings.

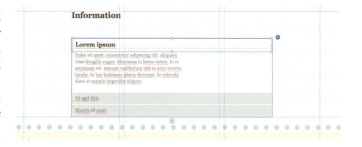

▶ Next, we'll change the Active label state's background. Go to the **Fill panel**. Set the color to *Warm Yellow*. Lower the **Opacity** to **60**. Finish off by setting the Stroke to **0**.

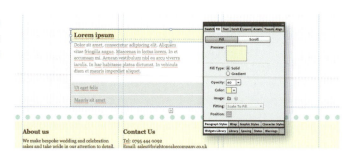

▶ Go to the **States panel**, or use the **States** menu next to the Selection Indicator in the **Control panel**. Select the Normal state. Click the *Label Active* paragraph style to apply it. We don't want the text to be bold here, so uncheck it in the text options of the **Text panel**. Duplicate the style. Name this one *Label Normal*. Remember to redefine the style settings.

Set the fill and stroke as we did with the previous state. Notice how the two remaining labels change as they are also in the Normal state.

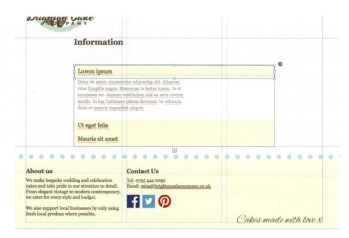

84

▶Select the Rollover state. Change the **Fill** color to *Mint Green*. We'll leave the **Opacity** at **60**. Mouse Down follows suit so we don't need to alter that.

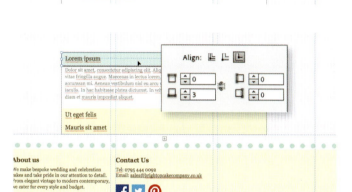

▶Currently, the labels have no separation. We'll create a divider by updating the Stroke width for the bottom of the label container.

Go to the **Control panel**. Set the Stroke **color** to *Chocolate Brown*. Open the **Stroke options**. Click the link icon in the center to unlink the four sections. Change the bottom Stroke value to **3**. Now set the Stroke **Alignment** to **Outside** by clicking the third icon. Repeat this for the remaining states.

▶Now we have the look of the labels set up, we can change the heading names. Double-click the first label text. Change it to *Menu and ingredients*. Do the same for the other two. Set the second label to *Portion guide*. The last label is *Pricing and delivery*.

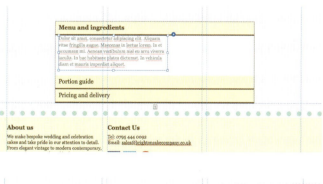

Populate the panels

We can begin adding our panel content. Click the *Menu and ingredients* header to open the panel. We don't need the sample text so use the **Selection tool** to select it, making sure the text frame is the active object, then press **Backspace** or **Delete** to remove it.

▶The panel content area has a thin white stroke. This acts as padding. We don't need this as we want to be able to fill the content area all the way to the edges. Click in the white area to select the Content Area object. Set the Stroke to **0**.

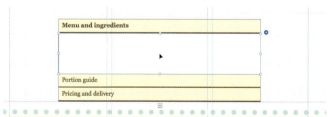

3 Creating the site content

▶ Each of our panels will have a banner image as a heading. Go to **File > Place**. Select the file *ingredients banner.jpg*. Click **Open** to load the place gun.

As we hover over the content area, its border turns blue. This tells us we're within the confines of the widget. Position the cursor in the top-left corner. Click once to place the image at full size.

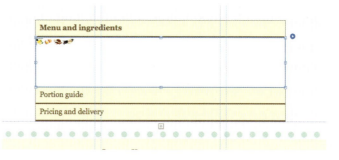

▶ Even though the banner image's dimensions are far greater than the content area, Muse has automatically resized it to fit the width. We can press the **Arrow keys** to make any small adjustments in the positioning, if required. Make sure that the top and left edges of the image frame are aligned to the edges of the content area.

▶ Next, we'll add the caption text area. We'll need to create some space, though. Select the Content Area object with the **Selection tool**. Drag the bottom of its frame down to open it up a little. At this stage, we don't know how large it needs to be; we can always resize it later.

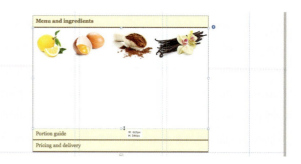

▶ Open the text file *information panels.rtf.* Select and copy the first paragraph under *Caption* (beginning *At The Brighton Cake Company*). Come back to Muse. Paste the text to load it into a text frame.

Drag the text frame up so it meets the bottom of the banner image. Now stretch it out to the left and right edges of the panel.

▶ We need to add some styling, of course. Use the justified *Page caption body* style as the basis. Go to the **Text panel**. Set the **Left Margin**, **Right Margin**, **Space Before** and **Space After** values to **10**. This gives us a nice border area for the caption.

Create a new paragraph style. Name it *Info panel captions*.

▶ Go back to the text document. Select and copy the text under the *Details* heading. Paste it onto the page as before. Stretch the frame out so the left and right edges line up with the caption text.

We'll use the rounded green container frame for the text background. Go to the **Graphic Styles panel** to apply it.

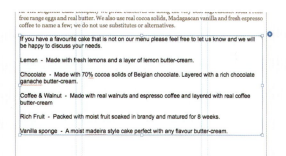

▶ Apply the *Footer Body* style as the basis for the detail text. Again, we'll make some changes. Set the values of left and right margins to **10**.

We can't use space before and after here as it will apply to every line-break. Instead, we'll use the old-fashioned method, adding a carriage return above and below the first and last lines. Create a new paragraph style named *Info panel details*.

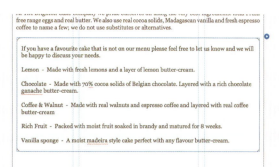

▶ We'll embolden the cake types' text to draw attention. Highlight each in turn, setting the style to *Bold*.

The final task is to close up the gap at the bottom of the panel where the text pushed it down. Grab the **Selection tool**. Make sure the Content Area object is selected. Now drag the bottom of the frame up. Leave a gap of around the same distance as we have between the detail panel and the caption.

3 Creating the site content

▶ The next panel is the *Portion guide*. Click its label to open it. Delete the sample text as we did before. The image for this section is *portion banner.jpg*.

When we place the image, it only fills half the width. This is because it's taller and Muse has inserted it proportionately. All we need to do is drag the right edge over. The image is automatically scaled up to fit. The content area snaps into position around the image when we release the mouse.

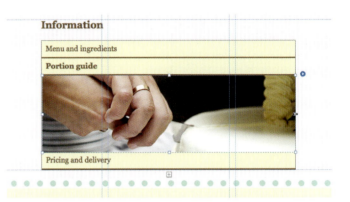

▶ Make some space below the image. Copy and paste the next caption onto the page. Align it to the bottom of the image. Stretch the frame out to the full width of the panel. Now apply the *Info panel caption* paragraph style we created.

Simulating tables

Muse doesn't support tables, which would have been ideal for this panel, so we'll need to create the detail section in a different way in order to divide the information into separate columns.

Start by creating a fairly large rectangular frame in line with the edges of the text and with the same distance from the caption as we did in the previous panel. We won't know exactly how tall to make the frame until the text is in place but, because it's just a background, we can adjust it later. Now apply the *Container* style.

▶ Go back to the information panels text file. Copy and paste the first set of data, including the heading, into the frame area. Use the **Selection tool** to position the text frame so it lines up to the top-left corner of the container frame.

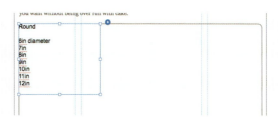

▶ Start by applying the *Info panel details* style. This gives us a 10 pixel margin on the left. To add a margin at the top, hold **Shift** and press the **Down Arrow** once on the keyboard. This nudges the frame by 10 pixels. Select the heading text and set it to bold.

▶ We can add a vertical dividing line using a selective stroke on the text frame. Set the Stroke color to *Chocolate Brown*. Now open the **Stroke options**. Set the Stroke **Location** to **Inside**. Click the link to unlink the strokes. Set the right Stroke's value to **1**. Drag the right edge of the frame to the left to shrink it to the correct size.

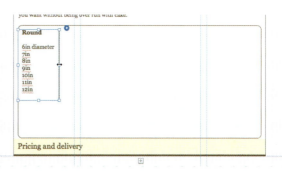

▶ Repeat the steps to add the rest of the infomation. We'll need to vary the widths of the frames slightly to fit the text. As the data is split into two blocks of three, we can align the far right frame to the right edge of the container. Remember not to add the stroke to the end frame.

▶ To complete this panel, use the **Selection tool** to drag the bottom of the container up to the text, leaving around a 10 pixel margin. Now we can drag the content area up, again, leaving a small margin before the third label.

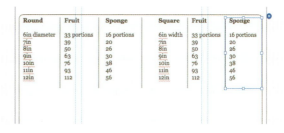

3 Creating the site content

▶ The final panel is the pricing and delivery information. This is set up similarly to the first panel, so I'll just run through the specifics of the layout.

Start by clicking the *Pricing and delivery* label to open the panel. Delete the example text. Place the banner image file *delivery.jpg* at the top of the panel.

▶ Extend the content area to accommodate the caption and details. Copy and paste the caption text from the *Pricing and delivery* section of the text file. Apply the *Info panel captions* paragraph style.

Each cake that we design and create is individual. The price is dependent on several factors. For example, the type of cake, the size and the amount of detail will all be reflected in the price.

▶ Copy and paste the body text onto the page. Use the *Info panel details paragraph* style to style the text. Now apply the *Container* graphic style.

Resize the container to align with the caption text. Add a carriage return at the top and bottom of the text. Make the paragraph section headers bold.

Finally, use the **Selection tool** to change the height of the content area.

Wedding cakes start at £250 based on a 3 tier vanilla sponge with minimal decoration.

Celebration cakes start at £65 based on an 8in madiera cake with minimal decoration.

Novelty cakes start from £100.

Deposits
A 50% non-refundable deposit is required when ordering your cake, the final balance is then due 3 weeks before delivery date.

Ordering
Ideally orders need to be placed well in advance. We recommend that you order your wedding cake a minimum of 2 months in advance. For all other cakes we recommend a minimum of 6 weeks. If you require a cake at shorter notice please contact us and we will see what we can do to help.

Delivery
For Wedding cakes, delivery and set-up are free within a 5 mile radius of Brighton. Delivery is free in the Brighton area on orders over £80. Orders under £80 are for pick up only. There is a minimal charge for areas outside of Brighton, please enquire.

▶ The last thing to do is remove the gray stroke from around the accordion widget itself. Make sure the accordion is the active object. Now set the Stroke width to **0**.

Each cake that we design and create is individual. The price is dependent on several factors. For example, the type of cake, the size and the amount of detail will all be reflected in the price.

Wedding cakes start at £250 based on a 3 tier vanilla sponge with minimal decoration.

Celebration cakes start at £65 based on an 8in madiera cake with minimal decoration.

Novelty cakes start from £100.

Deposits
A 50% non-refundable deposit is required when ordering your cake, the final balance is then due 3 weeks before delivery date.

Navigating the object levels

If you want to select an item that's buried beneath page elements, you can hold **Cmd/Ctrl** and click over the area to drill down. If there's only one object clicking again will toggle between the objects. If you are several objects down the hierarchy, pressing **Esc** will take you back an object at a time. This is often easier than trying to select them with the cursor.

Our services page

The page contains the company's contact details. Here we'll be using yet another of the built-in widgets, the Contact Form widget. This gives us a stylish way of adding a way for visitors to get in touch with the company with all the difficult data-handling handled automatically. The input fields are easily created with the options panel; we can make it as simple or detailed as we want, depending on the type of information we require back. We'll also be taking a look at the social media widgets section. Here we have several buttons and panels for including Twitter likes, Facebook comments, and other useful sharing options.

▶ To start, we'll create the heading on the page. Although it's easy to create it from scratch, we can use a quick cheat and copy the heading from the *Information* page. If we use **Edit > Paste in Place** (**Opt+Shift+Cmd+V**/**Alt+Shift+Ctrl+V**) it will be added in exactly the same position with the styling already applied. All we have to do is change the text to *Contact Us*.

Add a basic contact form

Go to the Forms section of the **Widget Library panel**. Drag the Simple Contact preset over to the page. It's more efficient to start with this and add what we need, than to remove the unwanted sections.

As with the other widgets, the options panel opens up as we place the form. We'll look at this in depth on the next page.

▶ We'll begin by adding a background for the form. Create a rectangle styled with the *Container* graphic style. Align the left-hand side with the heading. Bring the top of the container up to the base of the heading. Now hold **Shift** and press the **Down Arrow key** 6 times to create a margin of **60px** – the same as the panels on the information page. Stretch the right side of the container over to the middle column's margin guide. Position the form widget with a **20px** margin at the top and left to the container.

3 Creating the site content

The Form widget settings

The Form widget's settings differ from most of the others as they are split between the overall form settings and the individual elements. We'll look at the main settings first.

- **Form name** has two functions. The first is used to distinguish between forms that exist on the same site. The second creates the subject line for the email that's sent to the site owner. The name is initially taken from page name but can be changed to anything. Here I've altered it to Contact via website.

- **Email to** is the email address where the submitted form is sent. Here I've set it to the company's default email address *sales@brightoncakecompany.co.uk*.

- **After Sending** determines what happens when the form is submitted. The default is to stay on the page; a configurable message appears next to the submit button to acknowledge the form has been sent. We can also choose to display another page, a thank you message, for instance. Clicking the option gives us a choice of the site's current pages and history. We can also enter one arbitrarily. We'll use the default.

- **Standard Fields** are presets for the common fields we might have in a form, when enabled they are inserted into the form. Each has its own specific validation built in. BC CAPTCHA inserts the anti-spam field where the visitor is required to enter the sequence of letters which appears in the box above. Currently, this is only available when the site is hosted on the Adobe hosting servers.

- **Add Custom Fields** adds unique fields to the form allowing us to request information that's not included in the presets. We have two options here: Single Line Text adds a plain field the same as the default name and email fields. Multiline Text is the same as the default message field, to gather longer data submissions.

- **Edit together** is the same as the other widgets, giving the option to change the style of the fields in unison or individually.

When a form element is selected we can alter how it appears and behaves using its own options panel.

- **Require Entry** determines if the information is mandatory or not. The Name and Email fields are required and cannot be changed.

- **Show Prompt Text When Empty** displays a configurable message in the field if nothing has been entered by the visitor.

- **Label** toggles the display of the field's text label.

- **Message Text** toggles the text to denote a mandatory field. By default it's set to Required, but can be edited to display a custom message.

Styling the form

Form elements can be styled in the same way as the other page content. Select the Name form field item with the **Selection tool**. If we look at the **States Panel** we see that the element has five states. The first of these is Empty. This is the default look of the field when the page first loads.

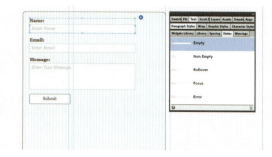

▶ We'll style the labels first. Click the Label item to select it. Use the *Footer body* style here. Change the **Weight** to **Bold**. All the labels now have this style.

I've also created a new paragraph style named *Form labels*. This prevents any unwanted changes if we decide to change the properties of either.

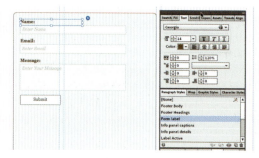

▶ Next, we'll change the look of the Empty field state. Click the name's text entry box to select it. Open the **Fill options panel**. Set the color to *Warm Yellow*.

Lower the **Opacity** to around **40**. We'll leave the text color at its default gray. Set the Stroke color to *Chocolate Brown*.

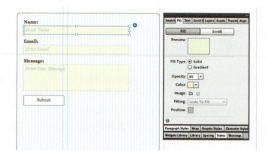

▶ The Non Empty state, as the name suggests, is the look of the field once the visitor has entered text. For this we'll use the same yellow but increase the **Opacity** to **70**.

This is enough to distinguish it, whilst keeping it subtle. Set the **Text color** to *Chocolate Brown*. The Stroke color is carried over from the previous state.

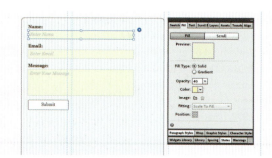

3 Creating the site content

The next state is the Rollover. This is the same as the menu items and links. The field changes as the cursor is hovered over it. Here we'll use a watered down version of *Mint Green*. Set the **Opacity** to **40**.

Change the text style back to **Italic**. Again, set the Stroke **color** to *Chocolate Brown*.

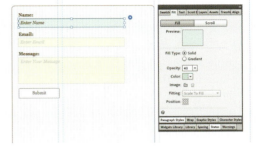

After the Rollover state comes Focus. This is the look of the field when it's selected, either via a click or tab. Here we'll make it a darker version of the green. Set the **Opacity** to **70**. Make sure the text style is **Normal**.

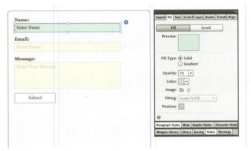

The final state is Error. This is used to highlight a problem when the form is submitted. This could be a mandatory field that's been left blank, failed field validation, etc.

The default is to highlight both the field and label text in red, as well as placing a red stroke around the field. This works well so the only thing we'll change is the **Opacity** of the field color. Set it back to **40**.

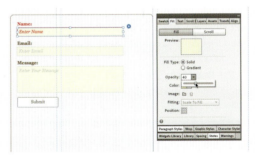

Now we have the fields styled as we want them, we can change the look of the submit button. Begin by setting the label.

We can use the *Form label* style but we'll need to make couple of changes. Set the **Alignment** to **Center**. Now change the **Leading** to **110%**. This places it on the vertical center.

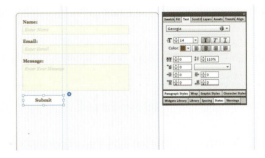

▶The Sumbit button has four states. These are almost the same as menu items. Select the Normal state. Change the Fill color to *Warm Yellow* with an **Opacity** of **40**. Set the Stroke color to *Chocolate Brown*. This is retained on all but the Submit in Progress state.

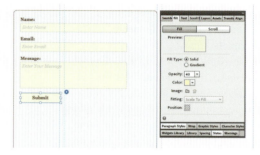

▶Next we have the Rollover state. Change the Fill color to *Mint Green*, changing the **Opacity** to **70**. We'll also use this for the Mouse Down state as we don't need a separate visual appearance for this.

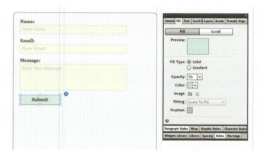

▶The final state is Submit in Progress. Set the Fill color to *Warm Yellow* with an **Opacity** of **40**.

Leave the text at its default style. You'll notice that there's an extra text field next to the button. This has its own states showing the progress of the submission. We'll look at this next.

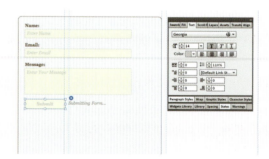

▶Click the text frame next to the button. We now have four more states showing. Ignore Normal. Select Submit in Progress. Apply the *Footer body* preset. Change the text style to **Italic**. Do the same for the Submit Success state. Change this to *Footer body* as well. Keep the style set to **Normal**.

The final state is Submit Error. This is set to red, which is OK. The default caption is a little frightening, so we'll alter it to the friendlier *Sorry, there's been an error submitting the form. Please try again later.*

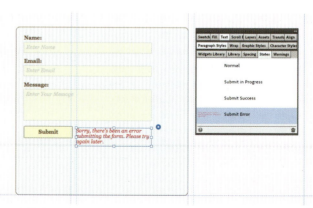

Creating the site content

3

▶ Now we have the form elements styled, we can add the necessary fields specific to the client's request.

Open the **Options panel**. Enable the *Cell Phone Number*, *Home Phone Number* and *BC CAPTCHA* options. Now click the Single Line Text option twice. The fields will appear on the page. We'll need to do some tidying up, of course.

▶ Click the *Home Phone Number* item, making sure the entire Form Field object is selected. Drag it up between the *Email* and *Message* fields. Use the Spacing guides to set the correct distance.

The form fields don't automatically move to accommodate changes, so we'll need to move the other items around ourselves. For now we can just move the *Message* field out of the way.

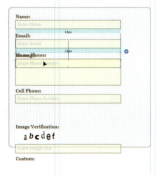

▶ Do the same with the *Cell Phone Number* item. I've renamed it to *Mobile Phone* as this is a UK site.

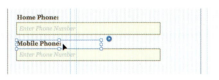

▶ Next we need to customize the two single line fields we added. The first is going to be for the visitor's location. Click the Label item to change the text. For some reason Muse creates these items with a very large gap between the label and the input field. Use the **Selection tool** to move them together. The presets have a **7px** gap.

Do the same with the second item. This will be for the visitor's post code (zip code for the US).

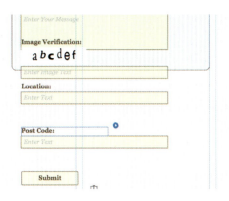

▶To save a little space on the form we'll place the post code field next to the location, since neither item's information should be that wide. To do this we need to first disable the **Edit Together** setting in the Form Options panel. Otherwise all the fields will resize at the same time.

Click the Location input field. Drag the right edge in to shrink it down. I've used a width of **226px**. Do the same for the Post Code field. This time set it to **100px**. Move both into position, side-by-side under the Mobile Phone field.

▶Move the *Message* field up beneath the *Location* and *Post Code* fields. Now move the *CAPTCHA* field beneath the *Message*.

The last item is the *Submit button*. My preference is to have it aligned to the right of the form with a slightly larger gap than the rest of the items.

▶To finish the styling we need to alter the background container. The form width is more than enough so we'll make the background narrower. Click and drag the right edge across to create an equal margin.

Now drag the base of the frame up to just below the bottom of the submit button. This will also allow us more room to have information on the right hand side.

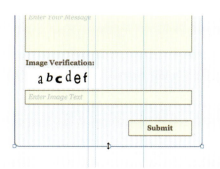

Testing the form

When we preview the form within Muse it's not possible to actually submit the form data, we get an error dialog. The validation still works, however. This is useful for testing purposes, as we (or the client) don't want to end up with tens of unwanted email messages. The form will work when previewed in the browser or when it's published, of course.

3 Creating the site content

▶ We need to change some of the form elements' settings to determine if they are required or not. We can't change the *Name* and *Email* fields, but we need to make visitors aware that they are required.

Click the Name item to make it active. Open the **Options panel** to see the settings related to that field. Enable the **Message Text** item.

▶ Select the entire form and open the **Options panel** again. Enable the **Edit Together** option. Click the **Required text** box. Change the text to an asterisk and color it red. Set the **Alignment** to **Left**.

Now move the frame over to the end of the field's label.

▶ Enable the message text for the email field. The size and color is already set as we are now adjusting the text boxes together. All we need to do is replace the text and move it into position, aligned with the field above.

▶ We don't need the phone numbers to be mandatory so skip them. Make sure the *Location*, *Post Code* and *Message* fields are set to required. Enable their message text fields and adjust them accordingly. The *CAPTCHA* field is mandatory by default, so add an asterisk to that, too.

▶ As a final step we'll add a legend to the form. Grab the **Text tool**. Draw out a text frame at the bottom of the form area. Type in ** Required fields*. Apply the *Footer body* style. Change the color to red. Align the text to the left edge of the form fields and the bottom of the *Submit button*.

Create a 'thank-you' page

When we reviewed the settings in the Options panel for the form, we saw that it's possible to redirect the visitor to another page once the form has been submitted. We'll create the page now.

Go to the site map. Click the plus sign below the *Contact Us* page. Name the page Thank you. We don't want the page showing up in the menu, so right-click the thumbnail and choose **Exclude Page From Menus**.

▶Double-click the page thumbnail to open it in **Design mode**. Go to **File > Place** (**Cmd+D**/**Ctrl+D**). Select the file *thank-you. png* from the *Assets* folder. Click once to place it onto the page.

The image is too large. Drag the corner handles to scale it down so the edges of the frame align to the content boundaries.

▶Grab the **Text tool**. Select the Alex Brush font from the web fonts section of the typeface menu – it may also be in the recently used fonts section. Set the color to white. Change the size to **72px**. Set the **Alignment** to **Center**.

Draw out a fairly large text frame. Type *Thank you*. Use the **Selection tool** to position the text. I've set it just below the top of the cake and in line with the back corner of the table.

3 Creating the site content

▶ Open the text file *thank you.rtf*. Copy and paste the first two lines onto the page. Change the font to *Georgia*. Reduce the size to **20px**. Set the color to white.

Resize and position the frame using the **Selection tool**. Align the right edges of the frame and heading. Indent the left edge so it lines up with left edge of the heading text.

▶ Copy and paste the next line onto the page. Use the same settings as before but change the size to **14px**. Stretch the frame to the same width as the previous text. Position it parallel with the top of the cake's stand.

▶ We need to make the word *here* into a link. Highlight it. Go to the Hyperlink menu. Select *Home*. This creates the link using the default link style.

▶ Open the Hyperlink options. Click the **Edit Link Styles** button. Click the **New Link Style** icon. Name the style *Thank you*. Set the color for Normal and Visited to white. Set the Hover and Active colors to *Warm Yellow*. Click **OK** to save the style. Remember to choose the new link style from the Hyperlinks options to apply it.

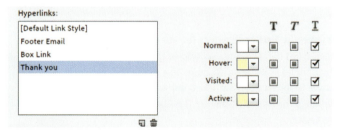

Set up auto-redirection

Now to set the page to redirect. **Go to Page > Page Properties**. Click the **Metadata** tab. Paste the code from the *Thank you* text file into the **HTML for <head>** section.

Go back to the *Contact Us* page. Open the **Options panel**. Change the After Sending setting to *Contact Us: Thank you*.

▶ The next part of the page is the information on the right-hand side of the form. Grab the **Text tool**. Draw out a text frame level with the top and a little to the right of the form container.

   Stretch the frame out to the center of the right column. We see the red guide appear indicating that the text frame is aligned with the right edge of the page area.

▶ Double-click inside the text frame to bring up the text cursor. Type in the heading *By telephone*. Set the base style to *Footer headings*. Now set the **Left Margin** and **Space Before** to **10**. Create a new paragraph style named *Contact info box heading*.

▶ Move the cursor to the end of the text and press enter to move onto the next line. Change the font **Weight** to **Normal**. Set the **Space Before** and **Space After** values to **0**. Type in the number: *07954 440092*. Select the text. Create a new paragraph style. Name it *Contact info box large*.

▶ The last section of the text is the business hours. Add a carriage return from the end of the telephone number. Type out the last paragraph as shown. Select the text. Change the **Size** to **16**. Create another paragraph style named *Contact info body*.

▶ Finish off by dragging the bottom of the text frame up a little to close up the bottom margin.

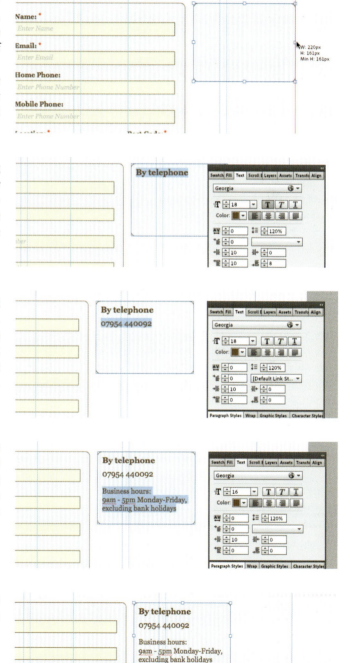

3 Creating the site content

▶The next box we'll create is for a Google map showing the company's location. Again, Muse has a built-in widget for this, which saves us a lot of time.

Start by drawing out a text frame below the previous box with an equal width. Leave a reasonable gap between the two.

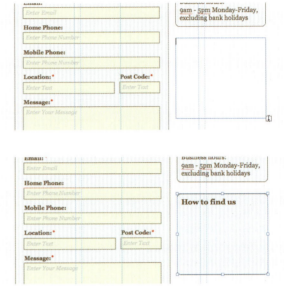

▶Type in *How to find us* for the heading. Go to the **Paragraph Styles panel**. Set the *Contact info box heading* style. Now grab the **Selection tool** to select the text frame itself. Apply the *Container* Graphic style.

Add a live map

Now to add the map. Go to the Social section in the **Widget Library panel**. Click and drag the Google Maps widget over to the text frame. The initial size is far too large for our design. It does highlight an issue, though: the map is going to be too small when we scale it to fit the container. This lets us see more of the surrounding area.

▶We'll scale the map to better fit the design. Drag the right side in, around a third larger than the container size will suffice.

Drag the bottom of the frame down so it's just above the bottom of the form's container, leaving space for the lower margin. The widget will refresh itself once we release the mouse.

▶Select the container frame. Drag it out so the map fits in with an equal margin. We need to alter the first box to match, of course. Click and drag the right edge over to align with the map frame.

Customize the map

We don't want the map pointing to Adobe, of course. Click the map widget to select it. Open the **Options panel**. For the address we simply enter the company's post code: *BN2 6TN*. As soon as we press enter, the map is updates to display the new location.

The pin information box is too wide to fit in the frame so we'll disable it by unchecking the **Expand Pin Info** option. Finally, we'll change the distance to zoom in closer on the area. A value of **15** is good.

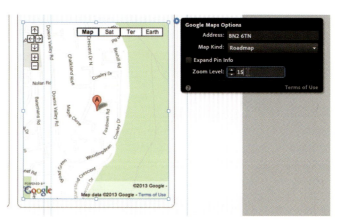

▶Since we had to make the text frames wider, the page is biased to the right. We need to adjust the position of the all the items.

Grab the **Selection tool**. Click and drag from the left side of the page heading down to the bottom of the map frame to select the items. Hold **Shift** to constrain the movement. Now click and drag all of the objects to the left.

Muse sees the selected objects as a whole, so when we see the red Smart guide to mark the center of the page, it's based on the alignment of the combined elements.

Google knows all

Whilst the postcode/zip code is the most efficient way of setting the map location, we can use other methods. The address field in the widget's options is a direct search link, so we could also enter the road name and, because the company already has an established site, we could enter the company name as the search criteria. This also populates the pin information with the data stored in the Google Maps database.

3 Creating the site content
Final adjustments

Increase the header margin

Before we move on, we'll make a couple of changes to the *A-Master* page. Go back to **Plan mode**. Double-click the *A-Master* page to open it in the **Design mode**.

The first change is an adjustment to the space between the header and the content. We can do this by dragging the header guide down. It doesn't need to be much, just enough to add more separation. Just below the bottom of the cake menus is ample.

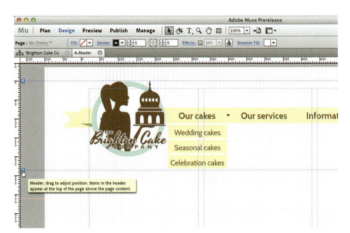

Add a footer site map

Next, we'll add a site map to the footer. This is useful for both search engine optimization, and provides visitors with a secondary method of navigating the site.

Create a text frame in the third column of the footer. Stretch it to span the width of the column. We can align the bottom of the text frame to the base of the icons.

▶ Open the text file *sitemap.rtf* in the Assets folder. Select and copy the entire block of text. Double-click inside the text frame we just created. Paste the text.

Highlight the heading. Apply the *Footer Headings* style. Now highlight the rest of the text. Apply the *Footer Body* style.

▶ All we need to do now is convert the text to links. Highlight home. Go to the Hyperlinks menu. Choose *Home*. Open the Hyperlinks options. Select the *Footer Email* style. Enter the Tooltip: *Home*.

Do the same for each of the remaining items; remember to only create links for the cake sub-pages.

The completed site content

That's our desktop site content completed. The additional space we added beneath the header has given the design valuable breathing space. Notice how the footer has remained at the base of the browser window, despite the varying size of the content. This occurs because the Sticky Footer setting in the layout section of the Site Properties dialog box. In the next chapter we'll be looking at creating a version of the site for mobile devices.

4 Designing for mobile devices

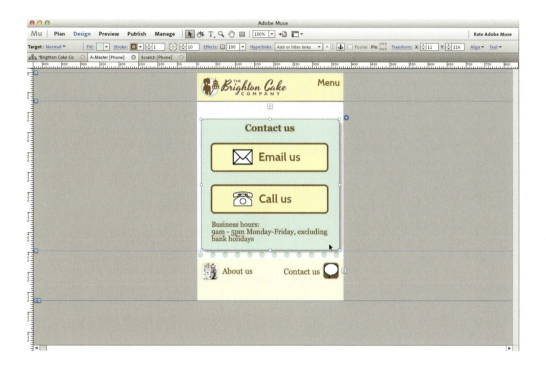

Now we have the content completed for the desktop version of the site, we can look at creating a version tailored specifically for mobile devices. Muse includes the ability to create alternate layouts for phone and tablet, so you can design mobile content specifically to display on mobile devices.

4

Designing for mobile devices
Creating the phone layout

Muse lets you create alternate layouts – one for cell phones, the other for tablets – dedicated to creating mobile sites. Each layout is preconfigured to fit devices, based on average screen sizes. When the site is published, both the desktop and mobile layouts are uploaded. The code detects the visitor's device and loads the relevant version. Mobile layouts should not be confused with responsive websites, however; Responsive layouts use style rules and called media queries to rearrange the layout dynamically.

In this chapter we'll be working with the Phone layout, as this requires the most thought about how the site needs to be altered to suit the space restrictions. Mobile sites, especially layouts designed to display on phones, are generally pared down from their desktop counterparts, providing only the most useful information in an easily read and accessible way. As we'll be largely working with the same content elements as we did with the desktop version, I'll concentrate more on the implementation here, rather than the technical side of constructing the pages; unless there's something new to discuss, of course.

Set up the workspace

Go to the **Plan mode**. Click the **Phone** tab in the **Control panel**. We see the **Add Phone Layout** dialog box. First is the **Copy From** menu. This gives us the option of None, where we would start with a completely fresh site, or our current desktop site. We want to base the mobile site on our current content, so we'll choose the **Desktop** option.

▶ We now have three options. The first is to copy the site plan; uncheck this. Although we're creating the mobile version with the same styling as the desktop version, we won't be creating an exact replica, so we don't want every page ported over.

Note: copying the site plan only generates the page hierarchy; the page content is not imported from the desktop version.

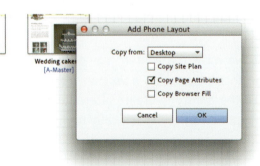

▶ We need to keep the **Copy Page Attributes** enabled, otherwise the dialog defaults to creating a blank site.
  Check the **Copy Browser Fill** option. A warning appears to tell us that the fill won't be visible unless the page content is transparent. Our site is based on floating content so we can go ahead and keep this option.

▶ When we click **OK** Muse creates a new site plan for the Phone layout. We have a master page and a home page, as we did when we first began the desktop version. The only difference is we start off with our striped background, rather than the plain gray. We could have chosen a blank site and set the fill manually, of course, but choosing to import the fill saved us a few extra clicks.

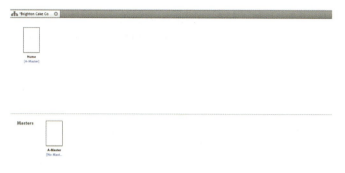

▶ As we borrowed the site properties from the desktop version, the home page is still set to be excluded from the menu. We need to make it available on the mobile layout. Right-click on the *Home* page thumbnail. Set the **Menu Options** to **Include Page with Hyperlink**.

The master page

As before, we'll start by designing the site master page. Double-click the *A-Master* page thumbnail to open it in the **Design mode**. There's no difference in the workspace other than the page dimensions, of course, we still have all the same tools and formatting options as before.

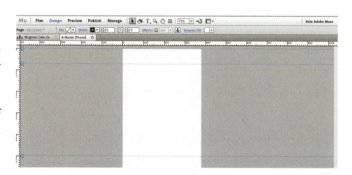

Add the navigation

The first step involves creating the navigation. This needs to be as compact as possible, whilst keeping its functionality. A good way to collapse a lot of information into a small amount of space is to use the Accordion widget.

Go to the **Widgets library**. Drag the Accordion over to the page. Use the **Selection tool** to align it to the top and stretch it out to fill the width of the content area. Remove its default stroke by setting the value to **0**.

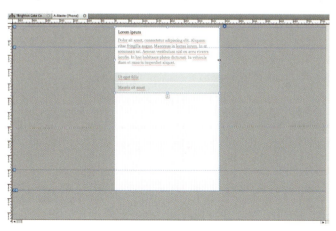

4 Designing for mobile devices

▶ We only need one panel to accommodate the menu. Click the first label to select it. Press **Delete or Backspace** to remove it from the widget. Do the same with the second panel. We're left with the single panel.

▶ Highlight the sample text frame in the content area and delete it. We don't need the panel background so set its Fill to none. There's also a stroke applied. Change its value to **0**.

▶ Go to the **Widgets Library**. Open the **Menus** section. We need a vertical menu here, so drag it over to the empty content area in the accordion panel widget. Make sure it's within the panel boundaries; the edges of the content area turn blue.

We can leave the menu settings at their default values. Click-drag the handles of the Menu widget to expand it, until it fills the entire content area of the Accordion. Now expand the menu frame to fill the whole width of the panel.

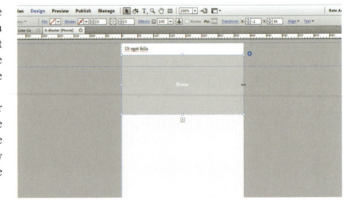

▶ That's the basics of the menu set up. We need to make a change to the accordion's settings before we continue.

Select the accordion widget. Open its **Options panel**. Check the **Can Close All** setting. If we don't enable this, the menu would always be visible.

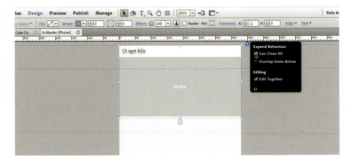

Style the menu bar

The next stage is to style the header and menu items. We'll begin by dragging the bottom of the label frame down to increase its height. Bring it down to the Header guide. This will be sufficient space for someone to tap the menu button, without the menu bar encroaching too far into the content space.

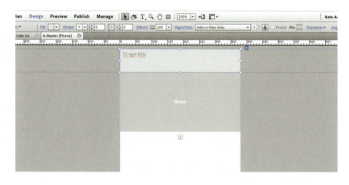

▶ Set the Fill color of the label to *Warm Yellow*. We'll also remove the default stroke and replace it with a single line at the bottom; this will help distinguish the menu and page content from the header. Set the Stroke width to **2px**. Change the Stroke **Location** to **Outside**.

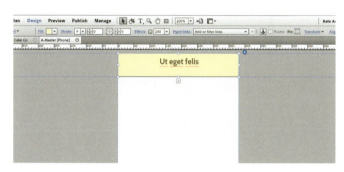

▶ Go to the **Paragraph Styles panel**. Click the *Main Menu* style to set the font to the same style as the desktop menu. Change the text **Alignment** to **Right**. We'll need to move the text away from the edge, so set the **Right Margin** value to **10**.

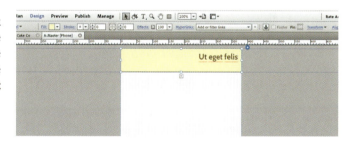

▶ Create a new paragraph style named *Mobile menu header*. This will prevent any accidental changes to the desktop version. Grab the **Text tool**. Click to select the label text. Change it to *Menu*.

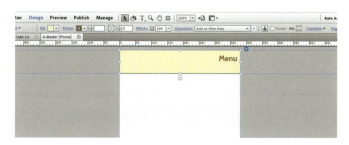

▸ Now go to the **States panel**. Select the Rollover State. Click the **Trash** icon at the bottom of the panel to remove the state setting. Do this for the remaining two items. This is a good technique to quickly unify the style of each state.

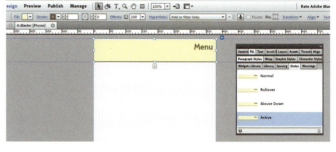

▸ Touch devices don't display the states in the same way as the desktop version; they cannot detect the visitor's finger hovering over a button, for instance. To show that our menu has been activated (and subsequently deactivated) we'll use the Active state. Select it in the **States panel**. Change its Fill color to *Mint Green*.

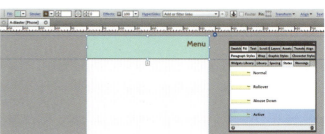

▸ We can create a Graphic style here to apply to the menu items. Click the Normal state to make it active. Now click the **New Style** icon. Rename it *Mobile menu*. This stores the style attributes. All we need to do then is change the active state to green after applying the style.

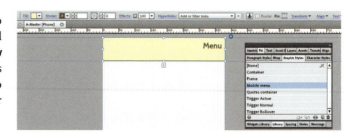

▸ Expand the menu (if it's not open already) by clicking the accordion label. Drill down until the Menu Item is the active element. Click the *Mobile menu* graphic style to apply it.

Change the Active menu state Fill to *Mint Green*. Now apply the *Main Menu* paragraph style.

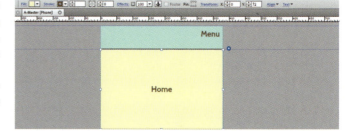

Keep tabs on your initial states

When you preview or publish the site, the initial state of the accordion, along with other widgets is taken from their current state in the design module. This isn't always a problem, the accordion on the information page for instance. If we were to leave the menu in its open state, particularly as it's defined on the master page, it will always start off open on every page we visit.

▶ To finish off the navigation bar, we'll add the company name and logo. Place the file *Mobile logo.png*. It's saved in the correct dimensions so click once to place it at its original size.

Position the logo vertically centered and on the left side of the header, 10 pixels from the edge.

▶ Everything looks great, until we open the menu. Because the image is a png with transparency, we see the whole of the green background.

There is no way of selectively changing the accordion's area without altering its content as well, so we'll need to use a workaround.

▶ The only part of the header we really need to see change is the area under the menu text. The rest can stay yellow. Grab the **Rectangle tool**. Draw out a box aligned to the left, the same height as the header.

Resize the rectangle, expanding it out to the right, stopping just before the menu text, leaving an equal margin area.

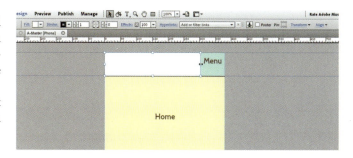

▶ Remove the rectangle's stroke. Now set the color to *Warm Yellow*. Go to the **Object** menu. Select **Send Backward** to move the box behind the logo.

This will keep the main part of the header yellow, as well as preventing the menu from opening by tapping any part of the bar.

4 Designing for mobile devices

Create the footer

▶ The next part of the Phone layout involves designing the footer. Start by dragging the Footer guide up. We'll make it fairly wide for now, it can be adjusted later.

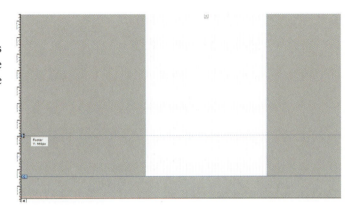

▶ Grab the **Rectangle tool**. Draw out a narrow (**21px**) frame across the full width of the content area for the divider band we used on the desktop version. Align its top edge to the footer guide.

Remove the stroke and change the Fill to the dot image, horizontally tiled. Make sure the **Footer** option is enabled in the **Control panel**.

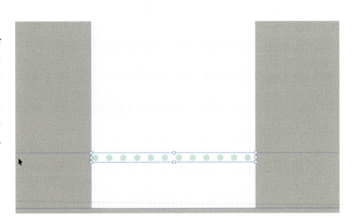

▶ Create another rectangle frame for the footer area. Remove the stroke. Change the Fill color to *Warm Yellow*. As with the desktop version, we'll drop the **Opacity** to **50%**. Again, make sure it's set as a footer item.

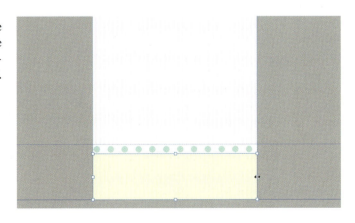

Pop-up information panels

Instead of having the company's mission statement and contact details listed directly in the footer area, which would either take up a lot of space or be too small to read properly, we'll create pop-up panels using a widget. This will give the mobile site a more app-like feel.

Go to the **Widgets library**. Drag a Blank Presentation widget onto the page. Don't worry about the placement just yet. Make sure it's set as footer item. You can right-click and select Footer Item from the menu that appears.

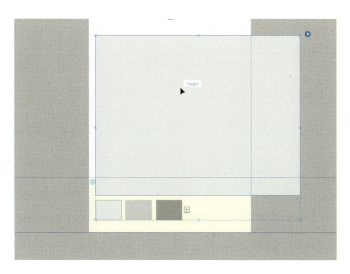

▶ We'll only need two buttons. Click on one of the triggers to select it. Now press **Delete** or **Backspace** to remove it from the widget.

▶ Open up the **Options panel**. Change the settings to the following (options not listed should be disabled):

Position: Scattered
Show target: On Click
Hide target: On Click
Transition: Fading
Transition Speed: 0.5 seconds
Hide All Initially: On
Triggers On Top: On

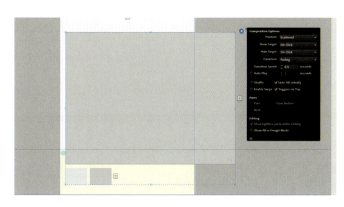

▶ Click the left trigger to make it active. Now select its target. Position the target container to align its top to the top of the footer divider. Drag the left edge to be in line with the edge of the header logo. Now drag the right edge in to create an equal margin. We won't adjust the height as we don't yet know how much space we need for the content.

Designing for mobile devices

▶Click the second trigger to activate its target area. Resize and position the frame as we just did. As we used the **Scattered** option, we'll be able to set the height of the content independently.

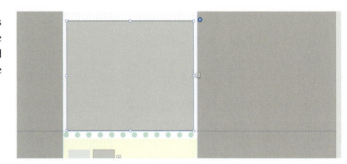

▶Now we'll set the position of the triggers. Click and drag the first trigger to align with the left edge of the target. Leave a small gap below the footer divider.

Do the same with the second trigger, aligning it to the right edge of the target. We can use the Smart guides to match the vertical position.

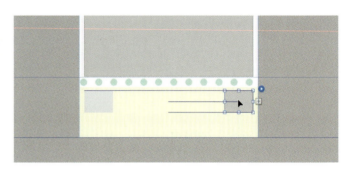

▶We'll set up the left-hand button first. This will be the company's mission statement. Go to **File > Place**. Select the image *about-us-button.jpg*. Click once to place it into the trigger frame. The image will be scaled to fit. Use the cursor keys to nudge the image frame into position if necessary.

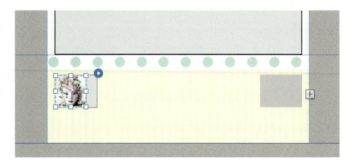

▶To make it look more like a button we'll add a rounded stroke. Make sure the object's state is **Normal**. Change the Stroke color to *Mint Green*. Set the Stroke width to **2**. Now change the corner radius to 10. Set the location to Inside.

Make sure the states are all the same by selecting each remaining state in turn and clicking the **Trash** icon in the **States panel**.

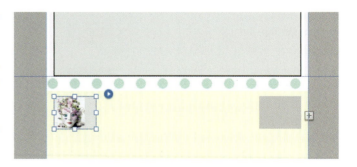

▶Stretch the right side of the trigger frame to make room for the label text. Grab the **Text tool** Create a text frame inside the trigger. Type About us. Select the text. Apply the *Slide Caption* paragraph style.

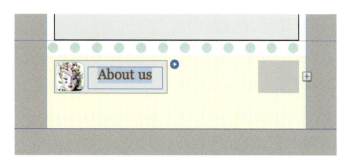

▶Select the trigger item. Set the Fill to *None*. Remove the stroke by setting its value to **0**. Set the other states to match. We can finish off by fine-tuning the position of the label.

▶Now we'll add the Contact panel. Place the file *contact-us-button.jpg* into the right-hand trigger. Add the green border as we did for the *About us* button.

▶We can make a duplicate of the About us label by holding **Opt**/**Alt** and dragging with the **Selection tool**. Change the text to *Contact us*. Now position it inside the right trigger. Finish off by removing the stroke and background from the trigger.

4 Designing for mobile devices

The About Us panel

Let's create the content for the two panels. We'll start with the About us section. Click the trigger to make sure we're selecting the correct object. Open the file *About us mobile.rtf*. Select and copy the whole block of text. Paste it into Muse. Use the **Selection tool** to drag it into the target area. Stretch the text frame out to fill the panel.

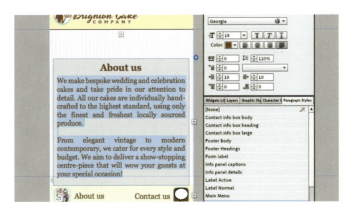

▶Highlight the heading text. Apply the *Page caption heading* style. Change the **Alignment** to **Center**. Set the **Space Before** value to **10** to create a margin at the top. Create a new paragraph style named *Mobile info heading*.

▶Now highlight the body text. Apply the *Contact info box large* style. Change the **Alignment** to **Justified**. Set the right margin to 10 to match the left. Create a new paragraph style named *Mobile info body*.

The text has pushed the target panel down over the footer. We'll be changing the style of the panel next.

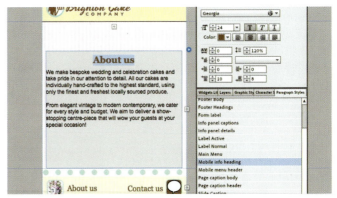

▶The next step is to style the panel itself. Select the target container inside the Presentation widget. Apply the *Container* style from the **Graphic Styles panel**.

We need to change the transparency as the panel will be overlaying the page content. Set the **Opacity** to **100**.

▶To add a little more separation for the panel we can add a light drop shadow. Open the **Effects** settings. Select the **Drop Shadow** tab. Click to enable the shadow. Change the **Opacity** to around **35**. Leave the rest of the settings at their defaults.

Create a new graphic style named *Mobile info panel*.

▶Lastly, we need to reposition the panel. Make sure the target is the active object. Press the **Up Arrow** key to nudge the panel so it sits just above the top of the divider bar.

Even though the panel is in the content area, because we have the composition widget set as a footer item, it will always appear in this position relative to the page when viewed in a mobile browser.

Designing for mobile devices

The Contact Us panel

Now we'll set up the Contact us panel. Click its trigger to make the object active. As we have the new panel style, we can apply it now so we have an idea of the space we have to place our buttons. Nudge the panel up a little by pressing the **Up Arrow** key a few times, as we did previously.

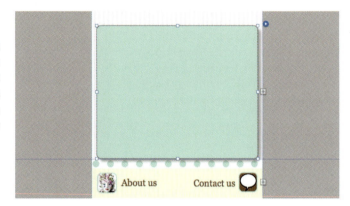

▶ Create a text frame at the top of the panel. Drag it out to span the entire width. Type in *Contact us*. Now apply the *Mobile info heading* style. The height of the text frame will automatically expand to accommodate the text.

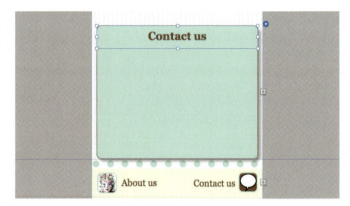

▶ Now we'll create the first button. Draw out a large rectangle just below the heading. Stretch the width out, leaving a generous gap either side.

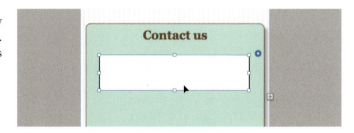

▶ Set the Fill color to *Warm Yellow*. Increase the Stroke value to **4** to create a border. Change the Stroke color to *Chocolate Brown*. Set the **Corner Radius** to **10**. Create a new graphic style named *Big button*.

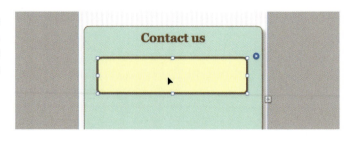

▶ Create a text frame inside the button; don't worry about the position for now. Type in Email us. Apply the *Main menu* style. Change the **Size** to **30**.

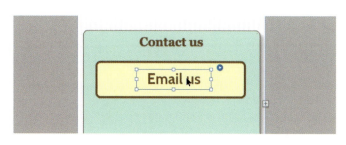

▶ Go to **File > Place**. Open the *Email.png* file. Position the cursor just inside the top stroke of the button. Click and drag the graphic out to meet the inside of the bottom stroke. Add some space between the image and the text.

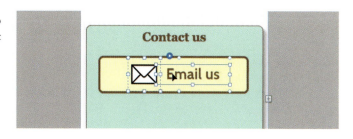

▶ Hold **Shift** and click the text to add it to the selection. Drag the label and its graphic so they're centered on the button.

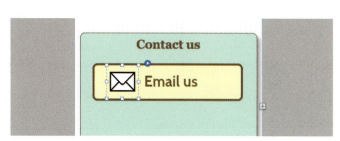

▶ Hold **Shift** again. Now click on the button to add it to the selected items. Hold **Opt/Alt** as well and drag the items down to create a duplicate of the whole button. Leave a large gap between the two. We need to ensure there's enough separation to make it easy to press on the device so the visitor doesn't activate the wrong button in error.

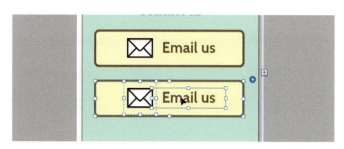

▶ Select the email icon and delete it by pressing **Delete** or **Backspace**. Replace it with the *Telephone.png* image.

Double-click the text frame. Change the label to *Call us*. We'll need to nudge the frame back a little with the **Left Arrow Key** to line the labels up.

Designing for mobile devices

Set up an email link

We have our buttons so now we'll set them up to perform the relevant action when they're pressed.

Select the button rectangle. Open the Hyperlink menu in the **Control panel**. Type (or select the link from the list if it's still there) *sales@thebrightoncakecompany.co.uk*. Press **Enter/Return** to apply. Muse will automatically convert the link to an email link.

Set up a phone link

Click the second button's rectangle. Go back to the Hyperlink menu. This time, enter the company's cell phone number: *07954440092*. Make sure there are no spaces or the link won't work.

When we hit **Enter/Return**, Muse adds the tel: prefix. This will prompt the mobile device to ask the visitor if they want to call the number; assuming the visitor's device is capable of doing so, of course.

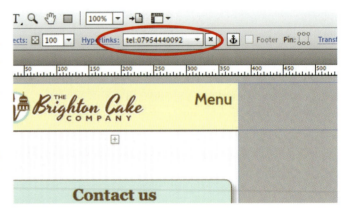

▶ To finish off the contact panel we'll add the company's business hours. We'll need to add some space at the bottom of the panel so click and drag the bottom handle down a little. Draw out a text frame with a width equal to the button.

▶ Set the paragraph style to *Label Normal*. Change the **Leading** to **120%**. We can either type out the text here or, to speed things up, copy and paste the text from the desktop contact page.

Don't forget to nudge the target object up to account for the additional space we added for the text.

▶ The final part of the master page is the company's slogan. Create a text frame at the base of the footer that spans the entire page width. Make sure it's not aligned with the base of the footer, as that may cause a gap at the bottom of the page.

▶ Set the font to *Alex Brush*. Change the **Size** to **30**. Change the color to *Chocolate Brown*. Set the **Alignment** to **Center**. Reduce the **Leading** to **100%** to keep the frame tight. Now type out the slogan text: *Cakes made with love X.*

Preview the phone layout

In Preview mode Muse offers us four preview sizes that correspond to popular cell phone screen dimensions,, so we can see how the mobile site will appear on a cross-section of devices. Left to right we have the Phone layout preview using the Apple iPhone 4, the iPhone 5, the Samsung Galaxy SIII and the Nokia Lumia preview options. The preview size options will no doubt change or be added to over time, as new devices appear on the market.

Designing for mobile devices

▶ Having completed designing the *A-Master* page for the Phone layout, we can begin working on the mobile site content. Before we do, however, we need to hide the info panel, otherwise it will be shown on every page as the page first loads.

Select the Composition widget. Open its **Options panel**. Uncheck the setting **Show lightbox parts while editing**. The panel will no longer be visible in the **Design mode**. It will still show and hide when the site is previewed and published.

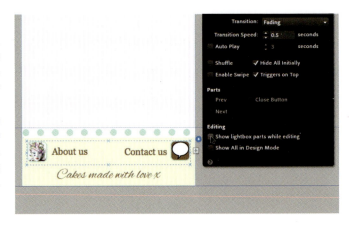

The home page

Go back to the site plan. Double-click the home page thumbnail to open it in the **Design mode**. We'll start by creating the slideshow; it will need to be slightly different for this version, of course.

Go to the **Widget library**. Drag the Blank Composition widget over to the page. It's far too wide at present.

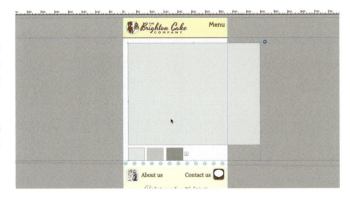

▶ Click inside the target area to select it. Stretch the frame out to fit the width of the page. Make sure it aligns right to the edge. Butt the top of the target up against the bottom of the header. Leave the height as it is for now.

Deciding on content height

We have to make a decision on height of the slideshow. If we make it too tall, the bottom of the content may not be visible on smaller screens. On the flip-side, if we make it too short, there's will be a lot of blank space on devices with larger screens. This is why it is important to test the Phone layout as we are designing it, using Preview mode.

Looking at the iPhone 4 preview, it seems like we can add a little extra to the target area but we need to take the browser frame elements into account. Any larger and we'll lose the bottom of the slides.

The triggers won't be visible on smaller devices but since the slides will automatically cycle, this isn't too much of a problem.

▶Delete two of the triggers. Highlight the remaining trigger. We'll keep the trigger size the same but resize the trigger container to make it square. Now we can use the graphic styles we defined for the triggers on the desktop version.

Open the **States panel**. Set each with the corresponding style preset. Apply the same style to format the triggers for the Rollover and Mouse Down states.

▶Click the plus sign next to the trigger to create a new instance. Do this once more to create the third.

Click the middle trigger to make it active. Move it into the center using the Smart guides. Now move the two either side, leaving ample space to be tapped by finger or thumb. In the sample project, they are 70 pixels apart.

We'll need to adjust the margin above the footer but we can do that later.

4 Designing for mobile devices

▶Now we can create the slide content. We'll be using the same images as we did in the desktop version. Click the first trigger to make it active.

Begin by placing the wedding cake image into the right side of target area. Scale it down to leave a small border at the top right and bottom.

▶Now place the flourished text and the confetti background. Remember to send the confetti object to the back so it displays behind the cake.

Now we'll add the call to action button. Go to **File > Place Photoshop Button** (**Cmd+B**/**Ctrl+B**). Open *call to action.psd*. It'll need to be a bit smaller than the desktop version so scale it down and move it into position centered vertically in the target and aligned to the center of the text.

▶Select the target container of the Composition widget. Remove the stroke and set the Fill to *None*. We now have the same transparent slide as we do on the desktop version. Repeat the process for the next two target containers to finish setting up the composition.

A shortcut to place the button in exactly the same position is to copy it from the first slide, then use **Edit > Paste in Place** on each of the others. We'll return to set up the links from the buttons once we have added the rest of the pages in the Phone layout, using **Plan mode**.

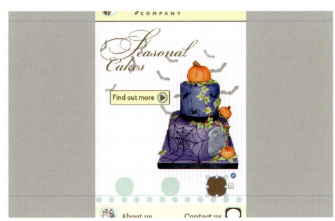

▶Open the widget **Options panel**. Set the **Transition** to **Horizontal**. Enable **Autoplay**. Make sure **Enable swipe** is also checked.

This allows the visitor to change the slides by swiping left or right, as well as using the trigger buttons.

▶We'll address the margin between the content and the footer. Go back to the *A-Master* page, either by going to the site plan, or by switching to its tab if it was left open.

Drag the Footer guide up by a small amount to apply some separation. Go back to the home page to see the difference this has made.

Fixing layout issues

Now that we have some page content it's a good idea to see how our footer content looks. Go to Preview mode. Click either of the buttons to open its panel. We have a problem! The panel appears below our page content when it should be overlaying it.

▶Return to the master page, enable lightbox parts in the widget's options. When we check the composition object's hierarchy, it's already at the top level. This is because the object order is made on a page-by-page basis.

As far as Muse is concerned, the master content should be at the bottom level by default. This makes sense, of course, and is generally not a problem.

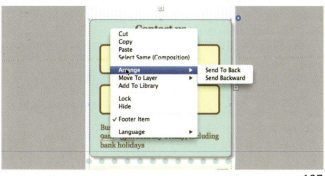

4 Designing for mobile devices

Working with layers

To rectify the problem with the info panels, we'll make use of Muse's ability to work with content on layers. Open the **Layers panel** by clicking its tab in the docked panel set. Or choose **Window > Layers**.

The concept of layers may be familiar to you if you've used Adobe InDesign, Adobe Illustrator and Adobe Photoshop. If you haven't used them, imagine building the content on a series of stacked clear acetate sheets that can be hidden and reordered at any time.

Here we have a single layer, which contains all of the master content. We can also see that the widgets have a sub-level hierarchy. We can drag the layers and sub-layers around to change their position – this is the same as using the Arrange commands from the **Object** menu, except it's more visual. The Layers panel also lets us see and alter an object's lock state and switch between the currently selected object.

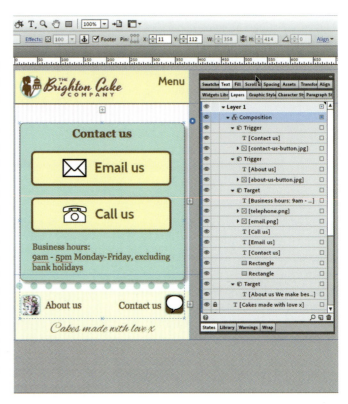

▶ To bring the panels to the front we first need to create a new layer. Click the **New Layer** icon at the bottom of the **Layers panel**. Our new layer appears at the top of the stack as *Layer 2*. Currently it has no content, so there isn't an arrow icon to expand the layer.

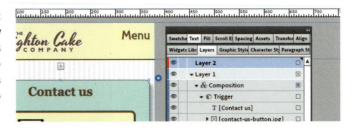

▶ Muse lets us change the layer name and its label color. This is useful as there's no thumbnail indication of its content.

Double-click the *Layer 2* label to open the **Layer Options** dialog. Change the name to *Info panels*. We'll leave its color as red; we'll see why the color is important in due course. We can also set the overall visibilty of the layer and also lock all elements on the layer simultaneously. Click **OK** to apply.

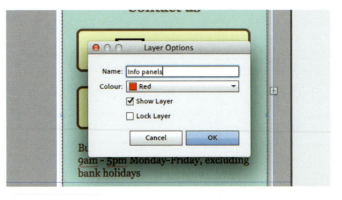

128

▶ Now we have our new layer, we can move our panel content. As with any application, there are a few ways to do this. We'll use the Object menu here. Start by clicking the Composition widget's label at the top of *Layer 1*. Go to the **Object** menu. Select **Move To Layer > Info panels**. We could also click and drag the object by its name onto the desired layer.

After a brief pause, the widget disappears from *Layer 1*. The new layer now has an arrow next to the layer name, indicating the layer contains content. When we open it up, there's our composition widget. Note that the widget's frame border is now red. This tells us which layer the object is on. All the elements of the widget will also display a highlight border in red.

▶ Set the widget option back to not displaying the lightbox parts to hide the panels. Go back to the home page. The *Info panels* layer is still at the top but we have no access to the content. This is because it's part of the master page. *Layer 1* is now for the content of the home page – here, it's just the composition widget.

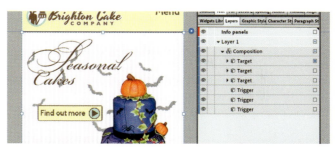

▶ Switch to **Preview mode** again. When we click the info buttons, the panels now appear above the page content. Our slideshow remains live, of course, and will keep cycling beneath the panel.

Although layers aren't always essential in the creation of sites in Muse, there are times when a particular layout or effect is not possible without them. They can also be useful in the design process, as they give us the ability to hide parts of the content selectively if we're working on a particularly complex layout. Just remember to turn them back on before publishing the site.

4 Designing for mobile devices

Our cakes page

Now that we have sorted the problem with the panels we can continue on with the page content. Go back to the site plan. Click the plus sign on the right of the home page to create a new page. Name this *Our cakes*.

▶ Double-click the new page to open it in the **Design mode**. We'll begin by adding the page title heading. Grab the **Text tool**. Draw a text frame across the width of the page, leaving a small margin beneath the header.

▶ Apply the *Mobile Type* style to the heading text *Our cakes*. The style attributes center the text and create a margin below the header.

▶ Instead of having separate pages for the cakes, we'll create a tabbed panel with a section for each type of cake. Each of these will have a short description along with a cutdown slideshow.

Start by dragging the Tabbed Panels widget over to the page. Align it to the far left against the bottom of the text frame. We can leave the default settings.

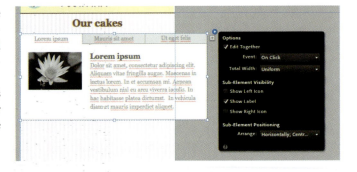

▶Before we style the panels, we'll remove two of the tabs. Drill down to the current tab object until the Selection Indicator displays the word *Tab*. Press **Delete** or **Backspace.**

Do the same for the next tab. We're left with a single set of a tab and its corresponding content area.

▶Highlight the placeholder content in the content area of the panel and delete it. We'll leave the width as it is for now, as the slideshow widget will stretch it out to begin with.

▶Click the tab object to make it active. Make sure the active state is selected. Set the Fill color to *Warm Yellow*. Go to the **Stroke settings**. Set the Stroke color to *Chocolate Brown*. Enable the **Corner Radius** for the top left and right corners to round off the tab.

▶Set the paragraph style to *Sub Menu*. Go over to the **Text panel**. Go to the font list. Choose *Cabin Bold*. Drag the bottom of the tab frame down to make it make a little taller. I've set it to **40px** here.

4 Designing for mobile devices

▸ Select the Rollover state of the tab. Change its color to *Mint Green*. Set the top corners to rounded as before. Set the paragraph style to *Sub Menu* but leave the **Weight** as **Normal** this time.

Do the same for the Normal state, setting the Fill to yellow. The Mouse Down state stays the same as the Rollover state.

▸ Click the content area to make it active. Make sure the Normal state is selected as this dictates the style of the other states. Set the Fill color to *Mint Green* and lower the **Opacity** to **40%**.

Finally, go to the Stroke **Width** field and type in **0**. This overrides the individual settings, removing the default stroke completely.

Create the slideshow

Expand the **Slideshows** section of the **Widget Library**. Drag the Blank Slideshow widget over into the content area. Leave a small margin on the left-hand side and below the tab.

We need to make some changes to the settings: set **New Hero** to **Fit Content Proportionately**. Make sure **Autoplay** is enabled. Uncheck all the options in the **Parts** section to hide them.

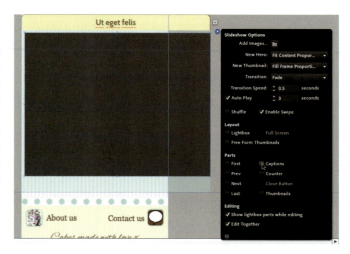

▶ Select the hero image object. Drag the right edge inside the panel so the margin matches the left side. Now drag the bottom of the frame down to make it a portrait sized rectangle.

Select the tabbed panel object. Bring the right-hand edge over to meet the edge of the page. Increase the space at the bottom of the panel; we're going to add a caption field here.

▶ Grab the **Text tool**. Draw out a text frame in the space below the slideshow widget. Resize the text frame to match the width of the Slideshow widget, leaving a small gap between the two.

Drag the bottom down just above the base of the panel area. Make sure the text frame is the active object. Set the paragraph style to *Mobile info body*.

▶ Before we start adding our content, we'll add back the two tabs we removed at the start. Make sure the Tabbed panel is the active object.

Click the plus sign next to the tab to create a new instance. Do this once more to create the third. This way we don't have to style them a second time.

▶ Go back to the first tab. Click the slideshow to make it active. Hold **Shift**. Now click the text frame to add it to the selection. Go to **Edit > Copy** (**Cmd+C/Ctrl+V**) to copy them to the clipboard.

Select the second tab. Make sure the content area is active. Now go to **Edit > Paste in Place**. The slideshow and text area are copied into the correct position inside the content area of the Tabbed Panel widget. Repeat this step to populate the third tab.

133

4 Designing for mobile devices

▶ Now we have the tabs and the placeholder slideshows in place we can add the content. The first tab will feature wedding cakes. Double-click its text label. Replace the sample text with the label text: *Wedding*.

▶ Make the slideshow widget active. Start by setting the hero image's Fill to *None*. Open the **Options panel**. Click the **Add images folder** icon. Browse to the *Mobile* sub-folder within *Assets > Wedding cakes*. Shift-select all four images. Click **Open** to start importing the files.

▶ We can reorder the images as we did in the desktop version. Open the slideshow **Options panel**. Enable the thumbnails. They appear to the left of the hero image.

Drill down to select the first thumbnail. Drag the thumbnail over the second to swap their places. We'll leave the rest in their current positions.

▶ In the **Options panel**, uncheck the thumbnails option to hide them. We're left with a panel that's too wide for the page. Start by selecting the Tabbed panel widget. Drag the left edge over to meet the edge of the page. The rest of the content is pushed to the right.

Now select the slideshow and the text frame together using **Shift**. Hold again **Shift** to constrain the movement. Drag the items back to the center of the page. Finally, select the tab panel again and bring its right edge in to align with the right side of the page.

▶Next, we'll add the caption text. Open the *Cakes mobile.rtf* file. Select and copy the block of text under the *Wedding cakes* heading. Make sure the caption text frame is selected. Paste the text into the caption text frame. The text is automatically formatted based on the style we applied earlier.

▶Repeat the previous steps to add the content for the seasonal and celebration cakes using their respective asset files. When all the content has been added, we'll need to tidy up a little.

Select the content area of the tab widget. Drag the bottom of the frame up, overlapping the text slightly. When we release, the content area resizes to fit.

You'll notice there's a large gap beneath the text on the Seasonal panel. This is unavoidable because the text from the wedding tab is longer and the panels have to be a uniform size.

▶Before we move on, we need to link the buttons on the home page to the featured cakes page we just created. Open the cakes page in the **Design mode**.

Drill down to the *Find out more* button container (rectangle). Go to the hyperlink dropdown in the **Control panel**. Set the link to *Our Cakes* in the Phone section of the list. Repeat this step to add links to the two remaining slides.

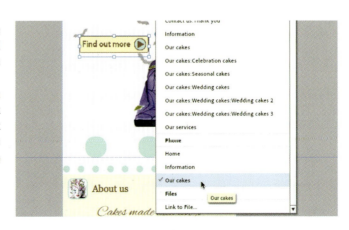

135

4 Designing for mobile devices

The Information page

The final page we'll create for the mobile site is the information section. Go back to the **Plan mode** to view the site map. Create a new page next to the *Our cakes* page. Name it *Information*.

▶ Switch back to the mobile site. Open up the *Information* page in the **Design mode**. Start by creating the page heading using the settings from the cakes page.

▶ Go to the **Widgets Library**. Drag the Accordion widget from the Panels section over to the page. Butt it against the bottom of the heading. Stretch it out to sit just inside the width of the page (see notes below).

   Remove the stroke from the widget. Delete two of the panels. Delete the sample text from the remaining panel.

▶ Click the label to select it. Change the state to Normal. Set the Fill color to *Warm Yellow*. Go to the **Stroke settings** panel. Click the link to unlink the four values. Set the bottom Stroke to **3px**. Change the rest to **0**. Set the Stroke color to *Chocolate Brown*. Set the paragraph style to *Sub Menu*.

▶ Go through each of the remaining states clicking the **Trash** icon to clear their styles. They will all be set to reflect the appearance of the Normal state.

Click the Rollover state. Set its Fill color to *Mint Green*. The Mouse Over state will follow suit. Now click the Active state. Change the font to *Cabin Bold*. We'll leave the content area set to a solid white fill.

▶ Click the plus sign below the content area to create a new panel. Repeat this to create a third.

Double-click the top label. Change its title to *Menu and ingredients*. Do the same for others, naming them *Portion guide* and *Pricing and delivery*.

▶ Click the *Menu and ingredients* label to open the panel. We'll use the same content as the desktop version.

Start by placing the header image *ingredients-banner.jpg*. The image will resize to fit the width of the content area. Make sure it's sitting just below the label.

4 Designing for mobile devices

▶ Open the *information panels.rtf* file. Copy and paste the caption text into the content area. Scale and position the frame to sit below the banner and span the width of the content area.

Apply the *Info panel captions* paragraph style. We'll need to change the font size as it will be too small for the phone version. Increase the size to **18**. Create a new paragraph style based on this named *Mobile info caption*. Highlight the company name and italicize it.

▶ Copy and paste the detail text into the content area. Align and stretch the frame out to fit the space. Apply the *Info panel details* paragraph style. As before, we need to increase the font **Size** to **18** for readability. Create a new paragraph style named *Mobile info details*.

Select the text frame. Go to the Spacing options panel. Click the link to allow the settings to be applied separately. Set the top and bottom values to **10**. This will give us an adequate margin.

▶ Due to a conflict with the container preset style we created for the desktop version and the pop-up panels (in this version of Muse, at least), we'll need to style the text frame from scratch.

Set the Stroke color to *Chocolate Brown* with a **2px** width. Set all four corners to rounded with the default **10px** radius. Change the Fill color to *Mint Green* with a **40% Opacity**. Create a new graphic style named *Mobile container*.

▶ We're almost done with the ingredients section; we just need to do a little house-keeping. Double-click the text frame. Select the ingredient names and embolden them. Select the content area, go to the **Spacing panel**. Set the **Bottom** value to **10px** to create a small margin.

▶ The *Portion guide* follows the same format. Click its label to open it. Place the *Portion-guide-header.jpg* image at the top. Add the caption text, styling it by applying *Mobile caption* style we created.

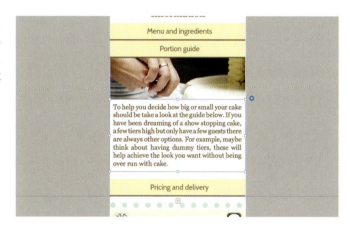

▶ The only main difference on this page compared to the desktop version is the portion details section. Instead of having the values side-by-side as we did with the desktop version, we'll place them vertically.

Start by drawing a rectangle beneath the caption text. Make it the same width as the text. Leave a small gap between the two. Apply the *Mobile container* style.

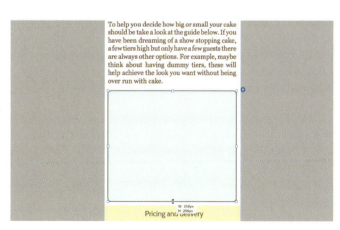

4

Designing for mobile devices

▶ Copy and paste the first block of information from the portion details section of the corresponding text file in the Assets folder. We'll use the *Info panel details* style here as the text will be too large with the mobile version. The visitor can zoom in on the text for legibility, if necessary.

Apply the *Mobile info details* style. Now go to the **Stroke settings**. Set the Right Stroke width to **2**. Leave the rest at **0**. Copy and paste the next section, styling and sizing accordingly. We have enough space for three columns.

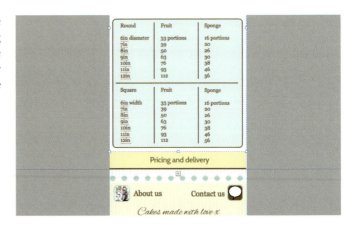

▶ Do the same for the next row to complete the panel. I've created a horizontal dividing line to separate the blocks. To do this, use the **Rectangle tool** to draw out a narrow rectangle. Set the Fill color to *Chocolate Brown*.

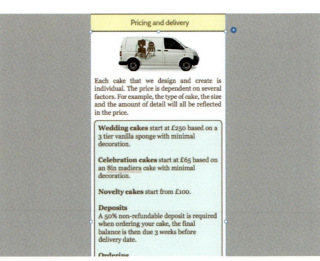

▶ The final section, Pricing and delivery, is straightforward. Copy and paste the text provided in the Assets folder as we did before. Use the same styles as we did for the ingredients panel. Remember to embolden the heading text.

All that's left to do is to shrink the content area up to meet the text as it was pushed down when the details block was imported. The bottom margin we added previously is carried over because the **Edit Together** option is enabled for the widget.

The section is fairly long, due to the larger text but it's a fair compromise for readability on the mobile version.

The completed mobile site content

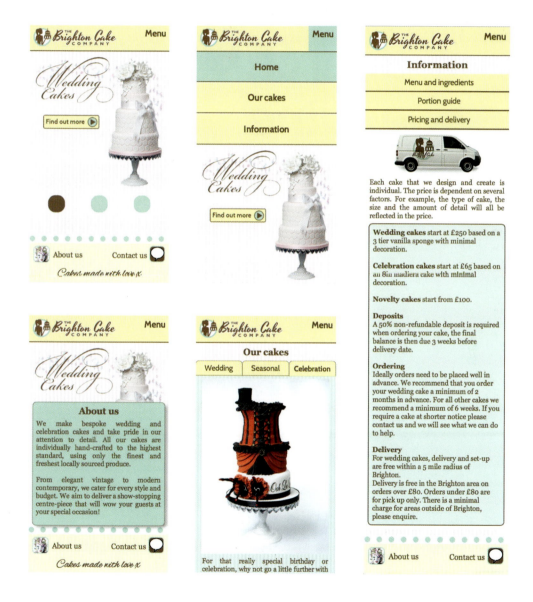

That's the mobile site completed, which also concludes the overall design process. There is the tablet layout to consider, of course. As it would be a hybrid of our desktop and cell phone layouts, there is no need to run through the details in the book. In the next chapter we'll delve into the world of search engine optimization.

5 Search engine optimization

In this chapter we'll be focusing on improving the ranking order of the site in the search results. As we'll see, Muse has some great behind-the-scenes tools for managing Search Engine Optimization (SEO), without the need to get buried in the code.

5 Search engine optimization
The concepts and practicalities

Search Engine Optimization (SEO) is one of the most talked-about things in the world of web-design, and with good reason. There's no point spending time crafting a website, whether it's for yourself or for your client, only to have it fail to appear in web searches.

It's far beyond the scope of this book to explain every nuance of SEO, of course, that would easily be a book in itself, and I am not an expert on the subject. In this chapter we'll be looking at the key concepts and how they are implemented in Muse. Many are handled automatically, such as generating a sitemap.xml file when a site is exported or published, and adding the detection code that redirects to the mobile layouts of a site. Others we need to spend a little time adding and tweaking our content.

There are many things to consider when optimizing a site. Below is a list of the topics we'll be covering.

- **Page titles**: the title that appears in the tab or window header of the browser.

- **Site description and metadata**: used for search-engine reference and displays in the search results for the site.

- **Page URL structure**: used for better site indexing.

- **Content and adding keywords**: helps search-engines find relevant search terms on the site.

- **Internal linking:** makes it easier for search engines to index the site.

- **Linking to social media**: visitors posting links to the site will generate incoming traffic.

- **Image titles**: file naming and text descriptions to boost search engine visibility.

Although much of what we'll be looking at here would generally be applied during site-building process, I felt it would be better explained separately to avoid too much information overload.

Setting the page titles

By default, Muse names the page titles based solely on the names we give them in the site plan. This is OK but it's better to have a direct association, both for search engine crawling and visual identification.

If we preview the site in the browser, there is no immediate indication of the site's owner or company. It's obvious if it's the only site open in the browser, but people often have more than one tab open at a time.

Muse gives us two ways of setting the page titles. Both are accessible from the **Plan mode** and also within the **Design mode**, depending on preference. It is easier to perform overall page-level amendments from the **Plan mode**, though.

▶ We'll begin by looking at setting the titles on an individual basis. Open the desktop site in the **Plan mode**. Right-click the Home page thumbnail. Select Page Properties to bring up the **Page Properties** dialog box. If we were in the **Design mode**, we could choose **Page > Page Properties**. Click the **Options** tab to open it.

Here we see options to set the page name. This is how it appears in the site navigation; although in this instance the page is excluded from the menus. Beneath is the page title. Currently, this is set to be the same as the page name and is not an editable field.

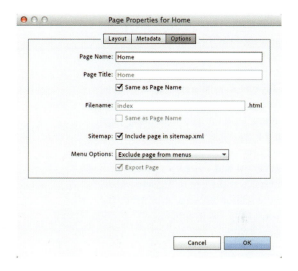

▶ Uncheck the box beneath the page title: **Same as Page Name**. We can now edit the Page Title field. Most sites have the name of the company as part of the title, often separated by a colon, hyphen or vertical line (often referred to as a pipe), which is my preference.

It's best to keep the title concise and relevant to the content. I've retained the original page name here; we could set it to anything, of course. *Welcome* would be a good alternative. Click **OK** to apply.

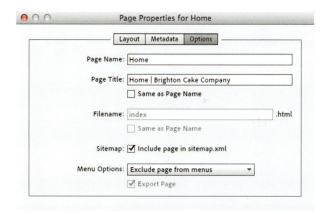

▶ When we preview the page in the browser again we can see how the page title provides a more descriptive title in the browser window. The company name will also picked be up by the search engines when they index the site, making the site more discoverable.

We could repeat this for every page in turn but there's a better way. Since we want the company name on each page, we can have Muse append the title text automatically. We'll look at this strategy next.

5 Search engine optimization

▶Right-click the master page thumbnail and select the **Page Properties** option from the menu that appears. Select the **Metadata** tab. At the bottom of the window are two fields. The one we're interested in is the Page Title Suffix. Anything placed in this field will automatically be added to every page title on the site.

Type in the company name preceded by the vertical bar and a space – remember to add the space at the beginning, too, otherwise there will be no separation from the page name. Click **OK** to apply.

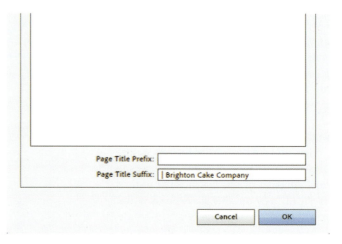

▶We'll need to go back to the home page properties and remove the title suffix we added. We can do this by simply checking the **Same as Page Name** option again.

When we preview the site in the browser, every page, including the two gallery pages we omitted from the menu, now have the company name appended to the name in the browser's tab/title bar.

▶We're still able to change the page names individually. For example, I decided to insert the word page to the name of the three wedding cake galleries. Muse still appends the text we set on the master page. Doing this doesn't affect the name on the navigation menu, of course.

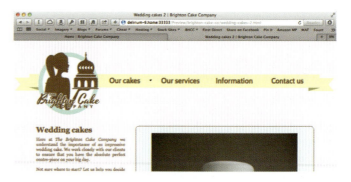

Before or after?

There is debate over which side of the separator the page name should be. I prefer to have the company/site name on the right; the page name is visually more important and risks being hidden if the text is truncated in the browser tab. It's also good practice to keep the page titles short and descriptive. There is little or no difference in how search engines interpret the title, other than the order in which it appears in the results.

Add the page description

The next task is to add a description for the page content. This is an important part of the SEO process, as it provides the search-engines with information about the site that can be matched to the search terms people are using.

The descriptions are created on a page-by-page basis. We'll begin with the home page. Open the page properties. This time click the **Metadata** tab.

▶Open the text file *description metadata. rtf*. Copy and paste the paragraph under the Home heading into the **Description** field in the dialog box. Click **OK** to apply.

▶Do the same for the rest of the pages, using their respective paragraphs in the text file.

The rule of thumb with the description is to keep it short, with as much relevant content about the page as possible. Try to avoid simply duplicating the text for each page. Here I've made the text as unique as possible, with the exception of the three wedding cake pages,

There's an unofficial limit of around 160 characters; there's no penalty for using more but the resultant snippet in the search results will be truncated.

Description:
The Brighton Cake Company will design, create and deliver a stunning, one-of-a-kind wedding cake to be the centrepiece for your most special of days.

Description:
The Brighton Cake Company will design, create and deliver a stunning, one-of-a-kind wedding cake to be the centrepiece for your most special of days.

Description:
The Brighton Cake Company will design and create a beautiful, one-of-a-kind cake for Halloween, Christmas or maybe just to welcome the beginning of Spring.

Description:
The Brighton Cake Company designs and creates stunning cakes to be the centrepiece for your special occasions. We cater to individuals and businesses alike.

What, no keywords?

Although Muse provides a space for entering keywords in the metadata dialog, there is little point in spending time entering them. Google and most other search engines no longer use keywords metadata as part of the indexing or ranking system. Instead, page relevance is taken from the title, description and page content.

5 Search engine optimization

Amend the URL structure

Another method that search engines use to index the site is by the page filenames. As with the titles, Muse uses the page names to generate the filename.

Open the home page properties. Click the **Options** tab. We see the filename is *index.html*. The option to change it is disabled, however. This is intentional: Index is the default page that web browsers look for when you type in the site address, if it wasn't present, we would have to specify the start page each time, so Muse prevents us from altering it.

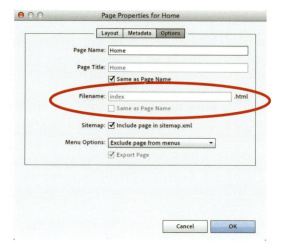

▶Most of the filenames can be left as they are, since they adequately describe the content. The only alteration I wanted to make was to insert the word gallery into the names of the image slideshows. This adds another useful keyword into the mix.

Setting the filename is the same as we did with the titles: uncheck the **Same as page name** option. Type in the new name separated with hyphens.

Click **OK** to apply the changes. Muse automatically updates the site content links with the new page name. Repeat this for the remaining gallery pages.

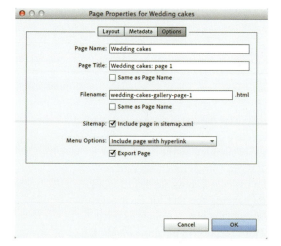

What's in a name?

Using the correct separator in filenames is of the utmost importance. Although it is possible to use underscores in the name, many search engines remove them when they are indexed. This means that the potential keyword value of the filename is lost. For example: *wedding_cakes_gallery_page_1.html* would be seen as *weddingcakes-gallerypage1.html*. It's unlikely this would be picked up as part of a search term!

Using spaces in filenames is another issue. Although it's allowed, they are not legal characters and are replaced by %20 when loaded into the browser. Again, this has a negative effect on keywording. Muse automatically replaces spaces with hyphens if you leave in the filename field of the page properties dialog.

Content and keywording

The most prominent data to be picked up by search engines is the site content itself. Writing copy that's relevant, and scattered with a healthy amount of keywords helps ensure the site is indexed correctly, of course. It's worth going through the site a couple of times to see if there's anything that could be changed in order to raise the page's profile. Ask a friend to throw some ideas at you; they may come up with a few terms and synonyms you didn't think to include.

It's worth noting that pushing the content too hard can have a negative effect. Overuse of keywords can be seen by search engines as spamming, as can intentionally placing misleading or irrelevant content. At best this would send you down the rankings. At worst, the site could be permanently excluded from the search results. Having text that reads *"Come to the Brighton Cake Company. We make great cakes, eat our cakes, enjoy our cakes"*, apart from sounding a little crass, clearly overuses the word cakes and could be marked down as a result.

If we paraphrase the text with something like *"At the Brighton Cake Company we take pride in our beautifully designed creations and know that you will find them just as delicious to eat as they are to behold"*, we now have a sentence with similar intent, without cramming in the same word repeatedly.

When somebody searches Google for a site like ours, that short sentence now potentially yields the terms *Brighton, cake, beautiful(ly), design(ed), creations, delicious, eat* and *behold* – depending on who's doing the searching, of course. It's also important to think about the company's demographic: who is the target audience for the company's services? Using plenty of synonyms in the copy helps to make sure you appeal to as wide an audience as possible. Keep that thesaurus nearby!

Create heading styles

As well as rich content, search engines pick up on headings, particularly if they're explicitly defined using HTML tags. We can do this right inside the Muse workspace.

Open the first wedding cake gallery in design mode. The specific page isn't strictly necessary but seeing the position and prominence of the text helps us decide how to set the tags. The page headings are obviously the most important. Go to the **Paragraph Styles panel**. Double-click the *Page Caption Header* to open the **Paragraph Styles Options**.

Use the menu next to the Paragraph Tag section to select **Headline (h1)**. H1 is used to define the most important information on the page. All instances of the heading across the site will now use this header tag.

5 Search engine optimization

▶ As well as the main headline tag, we have five more sub-heading tags. These are hierarchical, H2 being of second-most importance to H1 and so on.

The next level we'll define is the *Footer Headings* style, since it's used not only for the footer but also in the information boxes on the home page and elsewhere on the site.

Double-click its label to open the settings. Set the **Paragraph Tag** menu to **Subhead (h2)**.

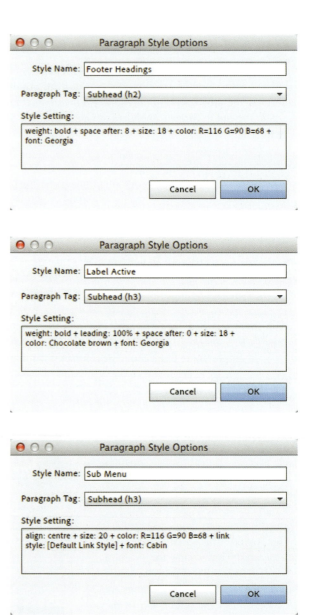

Paragraph Style Options

Style Name: Footer Headings

Paragraph Tag: Subhead (h2)

Style Setting:

weight: bold + space after: 8 + size: 18 + color: R=116 G=90 B=68 + font: Georgia

Cancel　　OK

▶ There are additional opportunities where we can apply paragraph tags to paragraph styles we've set up previously. The styles applied to the accordion labels, Label active and Label Normal, can be set to **H3**.

We also have a rogue heading style, *Contact info box heading*, on the contact page. We can set this to **H2** as we did with the footer heading.

Paragraph Style Options

Style Name: Label Active

Paragraph Tag: Subhead (h3)

Style Setting:

weight: bold + leading: 100% + space after: 0 + size: 18 + color: Chocolate brown + font: Georgia

Cancel　　OK

▶ We must not forget our mobile site, of course. There are fewer styles to set there but they're still just as relevant to search engines as they are on the desktop version.

Set *Mobile info heading* to **H1**. We can also add the tab and accordion titles. These use the desktop style of *Sub Menu*. Set this paragraph tag to **H3** as well. Click **OK** to save your changes and close the dialog box.

Paragraph Style Options

Style Name: Sub Menu

Paragraph Tag: Subhead (h3)

Style Setting:

align: centre + size: 20 + color: R=116 G=90 B=68 + link style: [Default Link Style] + font: Cabin

Cancel　　OK

Mind your head

There's nothing to stop you defining several instances of the H1 tag on the page, some content may warrant it. It might also be tempting to use heading tags to draw focus to content other than headings. It's better to use them sparingly, however, as search engines use complex algorithms to try and catch sites that abuse optimization tricks.

Create styles to define key phrases

To further help search engines pick up on keywords and phrases within the text, we can use character styles to define particular types of HTML tag, which draw attention to the content using the same strategy as the heading tags. There are several to choose from, some have more specific uses. Here we'll be looking at the two most commonly used: Italics and Bold (in HTML this translates to <em> and <strong>).

▶ We'll start with setting a style for italics. Open the first *wedding cakes* page. Highlight the italicized company name. Go over to the **Character Styles panel**. Create a new style. Double-click its label to open the **Character Style Options**. Set the name to *Italics*. Now drop down the **Span** tag picklist and select **Emphasis (em)**.

Although this has no visible effect on the page, behind the scenes, the code is changed to alter the way the style is applied by wrapping the characters with the <em> HTML tags.

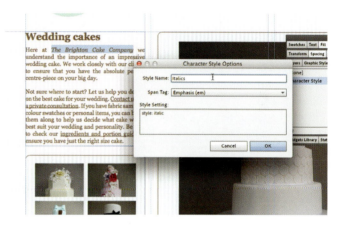

▶ The same technique can be applied for emboldened text. We'll use the content of the information page to define the style.

Highlight the word *Lemon* at the start of the ingredients list. Create a new character style as before. Double-click to open its properties. Name the style *Bold*. Open the span pick-list. Set this to Important (strong). In the background this will now have the HTML tag of <strong>, which will have a better chance of being indexed by search engines.

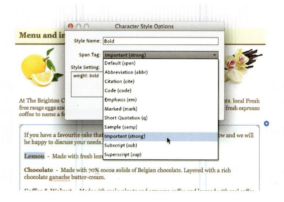

▶ All that we need to do now is go through the remainder of the site highlighting the text and applying the styles where required.

There's no guarantee that doing this will have a huge impact on the statistics but it's certainly worth putting the time in.

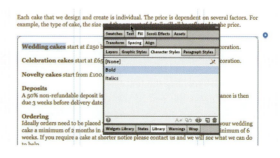

151

5

Search engine optimization

Internal linking

Internal linking is the practice of setting up hyperlinks to other pages within the site. Having additional links makes it easier for search engines to crawl the site and, since links are what search engines provide, it helps them to build up a more comprehensive map of the site. We've already provided internal links with the site map in the footer and the call to action buttons on the home page slides but we can go further. We can also place links in the body text to guide both the search engines and our visitors to relevant areas of the site.

▶ Adding links to the text may require a slight rewrite in order to make the link relevant. Here, I've edited the intro to the wedding gallery so I can place a link to the contact page.

It can be useful to set an entire section of the text as the link, rather than just the page name. This gives it more of a sense of purpose to the visitor, as well as squeezing in some more valuable keyword content to be indexed.

▶ We can also add more content in order to make linkable text. I've tacked on a sentence about ingredients and portion sizes so we can guide the visitor to the information page. The more often a page is visited, the more potential it has to feature higher in the search result rankings.

Remember to duplicate the new version and to copy it to the rest of the wedding cake pages.

▶ Links can also be more concise, of course. We can create links to the different types of cake wherever they are mentioned in the text. They are all useful for both the search engines and for guiding the visitor around; people may pay more attention to inline links whilst they are reading the text.

Once applied across the rest of the site, including the mobile version, we should be able to generate better page views.

What our customers are saying

Using social media to generate traffic

A good way of bringing traffic to the site is to give people the option to link the pages to social media. We already have the social media buttons in the footer but they may only be a one-way street; there's no guarantee that visitors will share the site in return.

Muse has built-in button widgets to most of the popular social media sites. We only need to put the buttons on certain pages; there's no point in posting a Facebook like to the contact page or having people adding the information page to Pinterest. We'll add them to the home page and the cake galleries.

▶ Open the Desktop layout of the home page in **Design mode**. Go to the **Widget Library**. Expand the Social section. Drag the **Pinterest widget** over to the page. Place it just below third info box, aligning it to the left corner of the box.

There's no setup for required for this version of the widget, it simply creates an overlay on the page showing the available images the visitor can pin.

▶ Next we'll add the **Facebook like button**. Drag it over to the page. Line it up with the Pinterest button, leaving a small gap between the two.

By default the button only shows whether or not the individual person has liked the page. Open its **Settings panel**. Change the layout to Button count. This will now show the total number of likes. Leave the URL as *Current page*.

▶ The last social media button is **Twitter Tweet**. This also shows the number of the times the page has been tweeted and also gives us default text to tweet.

There's a little more to set up here. Leave the Share URL at Current page and the size at Medium – the button will be the same size as the others when previewed. Change the Tweet text as shown in the example. Set Recommend to the company's Twitter account. Enable the **Show Count** option.

▶ Before we move on, we'll add the social media buttons to the Library. This means we can quickly copy them into the gallery pages without having to set them up again.

Draw a selection that encompasses all three widgets. Right-click one and select **Add to Library**. The item appears beneath the quotes object we created previously. Name it *Social buttons*.

▶ Open the first wedding cake gallery page. Click and drag the new library item over to the page. Place it just below the hero image, aligned to the left.

We'll make a small alteration to the Tweet text. Change the wording from *amazing cakes* to *wonderful wedding cakes*. This text description makes it more specific to the page. Do the same for the second and third gallery pages.

▶ Add the buttons to the remaining cakes pages. Update the Tweet Text fields accordingly, using the phrases *delightful seasonal cakes* and *spectacular celebration cakes*.

Targeting your demographic

It's well worth pausing to think about where your site is going to get its biggest audience, and not cluttering the page with too many buttons and links. Our cake company may do really well on Pinterest, as there is a large community of makers and crafters, predominantly female, who could be more interested in the content. Places such as Google Plus might not necessarily reach the intended audience. Muse makes it so easy to update sites that you can experiment with adding social media buttons and then check back in a month to see which ones are getting the most visitor interaction. Take care to remove the social media buttons that are not being used by visitors, particularly if they have a counter attached, as the Facebook and Twitter buttons do.

Adding descriptions to image content

One part of a website that often gets overlooked when it comes to search engine optimization is its images. The first thing we'll look at here is the alt text. This serves several purposes: if an image doesn't download properly, or in certain situations where the visitor may have disabled images in the browser, the alt text is shown in the place-holder. The text is also used to describe the image when screen-readers are used, often by the visually impaired. Lastly, the text is indexed by search engines, so we are able to sprinkle a few keywords in to help get our site seen.

Just like the file names of the pages themselves, the names of the images are also indexed by search engines. It's easy to select a batch of images from a folder to add to a slideshow but not really pay any attention to their file-names. There are tens of thousands of pictures on the web named *IMG_xxx.jpg* and the like, but far fewer, if any, called *seasonal-cake-easter-chicken.jpg*! The key assets for the site are already named but we'll see here what needs to be done if we rename a file after it's been placed.

▶ To add a description to an image, right-click on the image frame (one of the home page images here) and select **Edit Image Properties** from the menu. The **Image Properties** dialog box appears, displaying two fields. The first is the tooltip, this shows when the cursor is hovered over the image. We can use this for a brief description.

The second is our alt text. We can write a short description of the image here, including as many keywords as possible, of course. Keep the sentence fairly short and relevant to the image it's describing.

▶ We'll continue adding descriptions to all the main images on the site, including the site logo and heading banners on the information panels. There's little point in repeating myself and listing them all here; I've added everything to a text file named *image descriptions.rtf* in the assets folder.

When it comes to adding the descriptions to the slideshow images, remember to duplicate the text on the thumbnails as well as the hero images. Unfortunately, Muse doesn't do this automatically.

To help you decide how big or small your cake should be take a look at the guide below. If you have been dreaming of a show stopping cake, a few tiers high but only have a few guests there are always other options. For example, maybe think about having dummy tiers, these will help achieve the look you want without being over run with cake.

5 Search engine optimization

Renaming files

I mentioned using keywords for image filenames in the introduction to this section. This would normally be done before they are added to the page, of course. It's easy to forget to do this, or miss the odd file in a large batch when you're under pressure to finish the site.

There are two ways of renaming files: the first is to simply remove the image from the page and replace it with the correctly named file. This is OK if they've been placed as a whole with no adjustments but if we've cropped, or adjusted the image, or it's a single instance within a large slideshow, it can be a lot of work to remove and restore it in the layout, as well as needing to add the image properties text descriptions and tooltips again. It's much more efficient to rename the file that's currently in use and update its asset details.

▶ To illustrate this I've kept the original file names of the four images on the *Our Services* page. Open the **Assets panel** by choosing **Window > Assets** or by clicking the **Assets** tab in the docked panel set.

If we click to activate the first images, it will be highlighted in the list. We can see this is called *A6556997-Edit.jpg*: not the most common of search terms.

▶ Right-click on the file in the list. Select Reveal in Finder (or Windows Explorer for Windows). This will take you to the file location in the site's asset folder on the computer. Rename the file to *floral-face-cake-with-butterflies.jpg*.

▶ When we return to Muse, the item in the Assets panel still shows the original file name with a red warning icon. This indicates that it cannot find the original file. There is no automatic link between the two.

▶ To fix this, right-click on the asset again. Select **Relink**. Browse to the folder where the file is stored. Select the newly renamed file. Click **Open**. This updates the asset link.

We now see the item in the Asset panel with its new name. The red warning icon is no longer displayed.

▶ We can change the filenames outside of Muse, of course. If we do this before opening the site project, we may see a warning dialog to tell us there are missing files. We will also see them in the Asset list with the question mark symbol. We simply repeat the previous step to relink the file(s).

It is possible to multi-select batches of files to relink but they will not be actioned as a whole; a new file dialog will appear for each file. This can become confusing if there are many instances. If the wrong file is chosen, the asset will be replaced with it.

That more or less wraps up this chapter. It's worth going over the site and its assets again to ensure that we've covered every possible angle. There is much more to learn about search-engine optimization in general, of course; there are numerous books on the subject and a wealth of information on the web. Links to useful resources can be found on the book's accompanying website. In the next chapter we'll be nearing the conclusion of the project, where we will be looking at publishing the site to the web and setting up access so the client can edit sections of the site themselves.

6 Launching the live site

ow we have completed the website design and implemented the necessary adjustments for search engine optimization, it's time to upload the site files so that the pages can be viewed on the web.

Launching the live site
Publishing to the web

We've reached the point where we can publish the completed site to the web for all to see. There are two ways to do this: the first is to use the hosting credits that come with your Muse or Creative Cloud subscription. The second method is to upload the site to a third-party host, either through Muse, or by exporting the site files and uploading them manually using a separate FTP application. We'll be looking at both methods here.

Publish to Adobe hosting

The most seamless way to publish the site is to publish it directly to the Adobe hosting servers. To do this we simply need to click the **Publish** button in the **Control panel** or select **File > Publish**. The first time this is invoked, we're presented with a blank canvas. There are fields for the site name with additional options for selecting the publish location and data center; these are generally left to the defaults, as Muse handles them automatically.

▶ The name we give the site here sets the trial site's URL, which determines how it will be accessed before we assign its final domain name.

All trial sites published in Muse have a URL with a sub-domain of Business Catalyst, we're sharing it with everyone else, so the name must be unique. I've used *brightoncakeco;* this will need to be altered for the trial site you publish, of course. As we enter the name, the URL is automatically updated. If the name we chose is already in use, Muse will append a number suffix.

▶ Click **OK** to start the publish process. The first thing Muse will do is create the temporary site on the Adobe hosting servers – an email massage will be sent to the email address associated with your Adobe ID to confirm this.

Once that's done, the site pages and assets for both the desktop and mobile versions will start to upload. This may take a while in the first instance, since all of the site's assets and files must be published.

▶Assuming everything goes well, the web version of the site will open in the default browser. Muse also displays a **Publish Complete** message to confirm the site has been published. Here we have the options to invite people to be in-browser editors and also to associate a domain name with the site – more on this later in the chapter.

Both of these tasks can be done through the **Adobe Muse Dashboard**, so we could turn the dialog off by checking *Don't show again*, if this message becomes irritating.

▶After the site has been published initially, the dialog options change for subsequent uploads. The default Publish To option for trial sites in Muse is set to use the .businesscatalyst.com sub-domain. This can be changed, of course. We can also choose to publish to a sub-folder of the domain.

There is a new **Upload** menu. This determines which files will be published to the site. There are two options. The first, and default setting, is *Only modified files*. This is only uploads the files that have changed since the last time we published the site. This is the quickest method. The second is *All files*, which publishes everything, overwriting everything on the site. This is helpful when you have made a great deal of changes and want to update the entire site on the host servers.

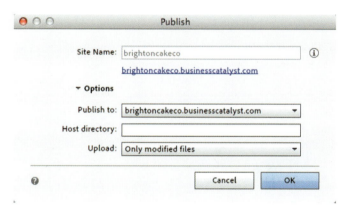

Third-party hosting

If you or your client already have a hosting plan with a third-party hosting provider, you can publish the site there instead.

Choose **File > Upload to FTP host** (keyboard shortcut: **Opt+Cmd+F/Alt+Ctrl+F**). We have a slightly more complex dialog here than with the **Publish** dialog box.

6 Launching the live site

▶ The first field, *Domain Name*, is required for associating the site to the Typekit fonts, the *sitemap.xml* file Muse generates for search engines and also to query the host's ability to run PHP scripting for the forms.

We would normally have a domain name associated with the hosted space but if the site's domain name has not been registered yet, this field will accept a placeholder name in the interim.

The *FTP Host* field is the address where Muse will upload the site. Again, this is usually a derivative of the site domain but the IP address can also be used.

▶ The *Host Directory* field is generally left blank, as the majority of hosting companies work on a single site per domain basis.

Some hosting providers, such as *Dreamhosts*, use sub-folders to define individual sites, so we would enter the folder name in this field, *brightoncakeco*, for example. Check with your hosting provider for their specific setup details.

The next two fields are for the hosting account's FTP login details.

▶ The *Upload* option is the same as we have for publishing to Adobe hosting servers. As there is no direct link to a third party host, we always have both options; the first publish operation is always All files, of course.

The *Store Credentials* option tells Muse to save the site details, including the login, to avoid having to type it in each time. Click **OK** to save your changes and begin the upload process.

▶ Something to bear in mind if you're uploading the site to a third-party host is form compatibility. After uploading to my host, I had the following dialog. I expected to see the warning about the CAPTCHA field, since it's currently only supported on Muse sites hosted on the Adobe hosting servers.

The second warning is because I'm using the company's current domain name, which is being hosted on a non-supported platform; it's unlikely that this would happen with a standard hosting platform. Again, if you have questions, you would need to consult your hosting provider for specific details about your hosting account.

Export as HTML

Choosing **Export as HTML (Cmd+E/Ctrl+E)** doesn't upload the site, instead it outputs the HTML files and assets to a custom-named folder on your computer.

You might use this option if you are unable to connect directly to your server through Muse. This might be due to company firewall restrictions, in which case you can use a separate FTP application to upload the files. You could also copy the files to CD or USB to send on to someone to upload the files themselves.

Click the location folder icon to change the destination. Be sure to create or specify a folder as Muse doesn't create one by default. Click **OK** to start the export process.

▶ After a short time, the entire site is created within the folder we specified. As before, Muse will display a warning about the CAPTCHA field in the form if it's not removed beforehand.

6 Launching the live site
Going live

In this section we'll be looking at making the site live and setting up the company's domain name for the Muse site hosted on the Adobe hosting servers. Third-party hosting is configured in a different way and varies from host to host, so you will need to read the documentation on their site or contact them directly to get details about your hosting account.

The Muse dashboard

The only way to open the site management tool from within Muse is to click the **Manage** button in the **Control panel**. A new tab or window opens in your default browser. This is the site management dashboard. The left column displays navigation to access areas of the dashboard, and on the right is an at-a-glance analytics and statistics display.

▶ In the middle section of the dashboard we have the web hosting information. This tells us what hosting plan we are using. In this case it's *Free Site*, the standard package we get with either the 30 day trial or paid subscription of Muse. The **Site Plan** section displays a button marked: *Launch Site*.

At present our site is private; the only way it can be seen is if we send somebody the trial site's URL. This is fine all the way through the design and testing phase when we can show the client the site's progress but no good when we want the world to see it.

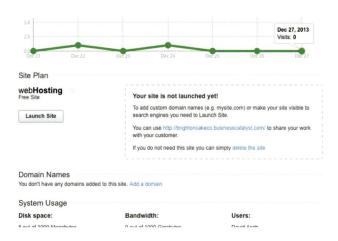

▶ Clicking the **Launch Site** button opens the Launch Site dialog box. We can see how many site hosting credits we have left. I have 4 out of the 5 that come with the full Creative Cloud subscription.

At the time of this writing, a standalone subscription to Muse includes one site hosting credit. Additional sites can be purchased separately, by entering a credit card and paying a monthly fee. Click the **Launch Site** button.

▶ Another dialog appears to confirm that it's now live. Currently, although the site is now visible on the web, the trial site is still using the same .businesscatalyst.com sub-domain address. Our next task is to assign a registered domain name.

This part of the setup can only be done if you have a domain name to add, of course. You'll need to register a domain name with a site registrar and pay a yearly fee to use it, when setting up your own sites.

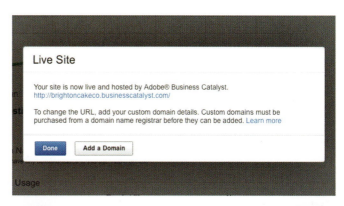

▶ Clicking the **Add a Domain** button opens the **Associate Existing Domain** dialog box, that contains a single field where we enter the domain name. This will need to be pre-registered with a domain registrar.

As the company already has a registered domain name, I'll be using it here. The www prefix can be omitted. Clicking **Save** adds the domain.

▶ Once the domain name has been added, the nameserver details need to be set up so the domain points to the site. A dialog appears with the DNS information for the Adobe hosting servers.

Information on how to set up the DNS records for some of the popular domain hosting companies can be accessed by clicking the *read more* link in the dialog. Alternatively, you can refer to the support section of your domain registration company's website. Click **Close**.

▶ Our new domain appears in the list of domains associated with the site. Note that we have two versions of the company's domain name: the first has the www prefix, this is the primary URL. The second is a redirect. This allows visitors to get to the site both with and without the www prefix. The remaining entries are the internal addresses used by the Adobe hosting servers.

6 Launching the live site
Creating a '404' page

Although visitors will usually navigate the site using the top-level menus or links in the footer, they may also bookmark pages to return to the site later. This is not a problem until the page name changes or it's removed completely. When this happens, the site displays an error page, commonly known as a '404' page, as that's the server error code for a page not found.

▶The default error page provided by the server is generally plain and unfriendly, and in some cases has no links back to the site content; this can be confusing and may result in losing page traffic.

We can create a custom 404 page that fits the theme of the site, with all the navigation included, so visitors can find their way back to the content they want to view. Even if the requested page no longer exists, it's likely that the content may have moved to a new page during a site redesign.

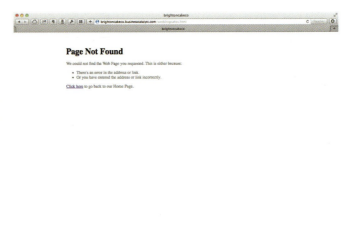

Design the 404 page

Muse doesn't have a built-in method of creating custom 404 pages, so we need to be a little creative. We'll begin by creating a new page to the top level of the site plan. I've added it to the right of the contact page. Name the page 404. We don't want the page showing up on the menu, of course. Right-click its thumbnail and select **Exclude Page From Menus**.

▶ The page will be similar to the Thank You page we created earlier in the book. Open the new page in **Design mode**. Go to **File > Place**. Open the image *page-not-found-png*. Resize the image and position it so its frame aligns to the outer page margins and sits on the Footer guide.

▶ We'll start by adding the heading text. Grab the **Text tool**. Change the typeface to *Alex Brush*. Set the **Size** to **72**. Set the color to white. Change the text **Alignment** to **Center**. Draw out a text frame next to the cake stand. Type *Oh dear!*

▶ Now we'll add the text for the error message. Draw out another text frame below the heading. Change the typeface to *Georgia*. Set the **Size** to **20px**. Type out the text:

There's something missing.

Please see the menus or the sitemap below to find the page you were looking for.

That's the page completed. Before we move on, we must publish the site again. This ensures that the image and CSS styles are present on the site.

6 Launching the live site

Enable online editing

We need to make a change in the Muse Dashboard to allow us to add the page content. Click the **Manage** link in the Control panel to launch the Muse Dashboard in the browser. Hover over your name on the right of the toolbar. Choose **My Details.** Scroll down to the bottom of the page. Now check the box next to *Enable online content editing.*

Although the option mentions that it's incompatible with Muse, this is only a warning that any changes made in the console will not be synchronised with the local site design file in Muse. Click **Save** to apply the changes.

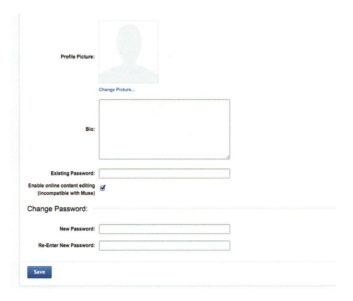

▶Click *Site Manager* on the sidebar. We now see a few more settings. Select *System pages*. We have two options here. Click the 404 Page Not Found link. This takes us to the admin page for the default 404 page.

Import the page code

We need to replace the current page content with the page we just created. Go back to Muse. Make sure the 404 page is open. Go to **File > Preview Page in Browser.**

We need the raw HTML code for the page. To do this we need to display the page source. This varies from browser to browser; for Safari go to the **Develop** menu and select **Show Page Source**. Highlight the entire block of code by pressing **Cmd+A/ Ctrl+A**. Right-click in the window and select **Copy** to save it to the clipboard**.**

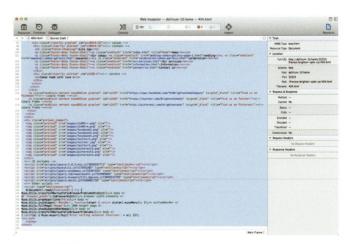

▶ Now we have the source code stored on the clipboard we can use it for our system page. Go back to the **Muse Dashboard**. At the bottom of the window there are two tabs: Design and HTML. Click the **HTML** tab to activate the window.

Highlight and delete the current code in the **System Message Content** field. Now right-click inside the field and select **paste**. The 404 page for the site will now use the the code that we copied from the browser.

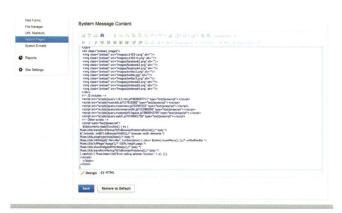

▶ Click **Save** at the bottom of the window. This stores the new code to the site. Once saved, the window switches back to design mode. Don't worry if it looks broken at the moment, this is just the raw page without its CSS styling.

Test the error page

All we need to do now is test that our custom error page is working. Launch the live site. Go to the address bar of the browser. Tack on a non-existent page name, */weddingcakes.html* for example. Press Enter. All being well, we see the new page displayed.

Remember to update

Any changes we make to the master template of the site, such as additional menus or alterations to the footer won't be reflected in the 404 page, as it's taken from a snapshot of the design. This can cause layout issues so make sure you remember to preview and replace the page code after publishing your updates.

6 Launching the live site
In-browser editing

One sought-after feature when creating sites is giving the client the ability to edit the content. Although Muse doesn't have a complete content management system (CMS), such as you'd find with platforms like Wordpress or Drupal, it does allow the client to alter text and replace images across the site, via the Muse Dashboard, using any browser with an Internet connection. Here we'll be looking at how to set up site users and how the editing system works.

Add a site user

Adding site users is done via the **Muse Dashboard**, which can be launched from within Muse either from the **Manage** option on the toolbar, or by selecting **Add In-Browser Editing User** from the File menu. Users can also append */admin* to the site address in the browser. From here we can either click the *Invite customers* link from the dashboard, which takes us directly to the setup panel, or from the *Admin Users* section of the **Site Settings** menu (shown here). This option shows us all users of the site, currently this is only the site designer.

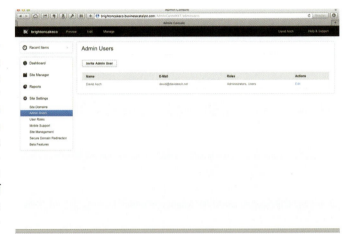

▶ Click the **Invite Admin User** button. A new panel opens containing the setup details.

First we have the email address, this must be valid as it's where the user's invitation is sent. This is followed by the person's first and last name, which will be how the user appears in the console. We can also add the person's cell phone number, this is optional.

The final section is the User Roles. This determines what the person can do both on the site and within the admin console. The *Users* role has been designed to allow most site editing functions and access to the site's visitor and usage statistics. If you're adding another designer to work on the site, use the *Administrators* role.

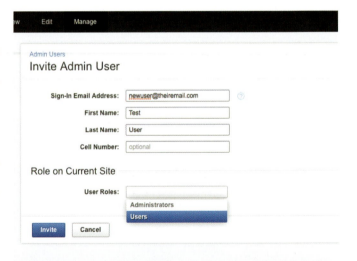

▶Once the user's details have been filled in, click the **Invite** button to add the account to the site and send out the invitation email.

When the email is received, clicking the link will open a welcome page where the user can create a password.

After accepting the terms and conditions, clicking continue will log the person into the **Muse Dashboard**.

Edit live content

Once logged in, the version of the Muse Dashboard the new user sees is almost identical to the view we have as site designers. Some of the site options are missing, of course, due to the permissions restrictions.

The section we're most interested in, of course, is the in-browser editing. To switch to edit mode click the **Edit** button at the top of the window. Our site is loaded into the browser window.

Apart from having the dashboard interfacebar at the top and a new bar at the bottom, there appears to be no difference between this and the normal view of the live site.

▶When we hover over sections of the page content, however, the difference is immediately apparent. Blue frames appear, highlighting text and images. Under these frames are edit buttons. These denote the areas of the site that can be edited.

Notice that not everything shows as highlighted. Site layout elements such as background images set as fills for image frames, text frames, and rectangles and automatically generated menus cannot be changed. The Photoshop buttons in the footer are also off-limits, as it would be too complicated to implement into the interface. Almost everything else is fair game.

6 Launching the live site

Change the text

We'll begin by editing the content of the *What's new* section. Use the **Edit** button or click inside the blue rectangle. The **Edit Content** dialog with the text from the text frame appears in front of the rendered site.

We can amend or change the text as we see fit, although care needs to be taken as to how much text is added. The way these text frames are constructed means that the text spills out, rather than pushing the content down as it does when you edit the site in the Muse workspace. This can be remedied by changing the layout, of course.

It's in our interest as designers to instruct new users that they should attempt to match the amount of new content to avoid layout problems.

▶Click the **Update** button to apply the changes. The content of the text frame updates to display our new text. This won't show up on the live site yet, however, what we see here is a cached version of the page, we can make as many alterations as we like before publishing the changes.

Replace an image

The next change we'll make is the image in the *What's new* section as it was only relevant to the original text. This highlights one of the constraints of the editing system, we're not able to remove image frames, only change them.

Click the **Edit** button or click the image. This time, instead of an Edit Content dialog box, the Edit Image dialog box appears. From here we can either choose one of the existing images on the site, or upload one from the computer. The cropped face works well. Click **Update** to apply the changes.

▶The *Events* section also needs amending. The original content is made up of two frames. Click to edit the top frame. Don't delete the existing text, though.

Currently, there's no way of adding a style to text within the **Edit Content** dialog box. We can, however, use the existing styles applied to page content. Highlight the date. Now replace the text with *Cake Classes*. Although we don't see any difference now, when we update it, the text frame will inherit the bold styling. Add the remainder of the text and click **Update.**

▶The only thing we can do with the second block of text is delete its content. Again, this will need to be altered in Muse to allow for proper editing by the user.

Click **Update** apply the changes. The second block is gone and we can see the *Bold* style has been applied to the sub-heading. This workaround works with almost all the text styles, including pre-defined paragraph and character styles.

Publishing the changes

Before we can move on to edit more of the site we need to publish the current changes – Muse will warn us if we attempt to navigate away from the page or close the browser window. Click the **Publish** button at the bottom of the page. After a short time a panel will display a message confirming that the changes are live.

We can click the **Preview mode** button on the toolbar to make sure the changes were applied to the site.

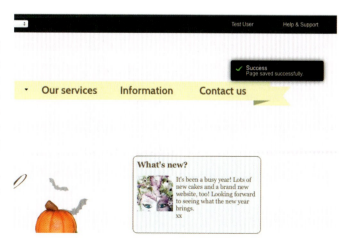

6 Launching the live site

Edit alternate versions

As well as the main desktop pages, we can also edit the mobile versions of the site. To switch to the phone layout, use the **Devices** menu at the top of the window. The desktop site is replaced with a rendering of the alternate phone layout. The editing process is the same as for the desktop site, just roll over the images and text to highlight them.

▶ A feature of In-Browser Editing is that we can roll over sub-elements of widgets and choose whether to edit the sub-element or click it to see the associated content. Since they have editable text and also need to be clicked to activate them, we need to be able to make the distinction.

The menu has been set up using a widget, when we hover over the item, we now have two choices: **edit** and **click**. Choosing **Click** activates the menu as it would if we were navigating the page in a browser, choosing **Edit** opens the text editor enabling us to alter the label text.

Update changes in Muse

When changes are made on the live website, they need to be reflected in Muse to avoid future conflicts. As soon as we reopen the site in Muse, it detects if any changes were made using In-Browser Editing. If there are, the **Review and Merge Changes** dialog box appears, allowing us to review and merge or discard the alterations.

The item in question is highlighted on the page. We can also choose to see the change in place by checking **Preview on page.** The menus on the **Merge** and **Merge into Muse** buttons allow us to step through each change or to use the chosen option for all remaining items.

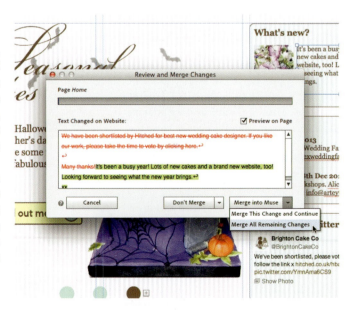

Adding a 'favicon'

As a final garnish to the newly published site, we'll create the icon that sits next to the address in the browser, known as the *favicon*. Without setting one up the browser uses its default image, in Safari's case, this is a blue globe.

▶ Select **File > Site Properties**. Click the folder icon next to Favicon image at the bottom of the Layout panel. Browse to select the file *favicon.png*. The image appears in the square to the left. This is its actual size. Click **OK** to set the changes.

If you search the web for the term Favicon, you'll find many free Favicon generators online that enable you to upload a square image file and then download the resized image that you can add to the site.

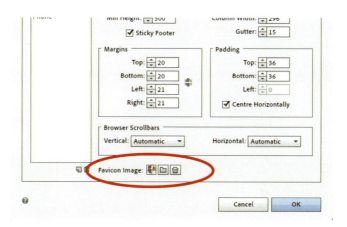

▶ Click the **Publish** button to upload the latest version of the site. When the browser opens we can see our new icon next to the address. Although it's not essential to do this, it does look a lot nicer than the browser default and it does help to distinguish the site from others in your bookmarks.

Favicons also appear in the browser's tab when the visitor has more than one page open at a time, also helping to distinguish the site.

So that's the site live and ready to be seen by the world. All that remains is to make sure people know about it. Search-engine optimization works but it's going to need help. Word-of-mouth, business cards and links from other sites are all vital to generating traffic and ultimately increasing traffic to the site.

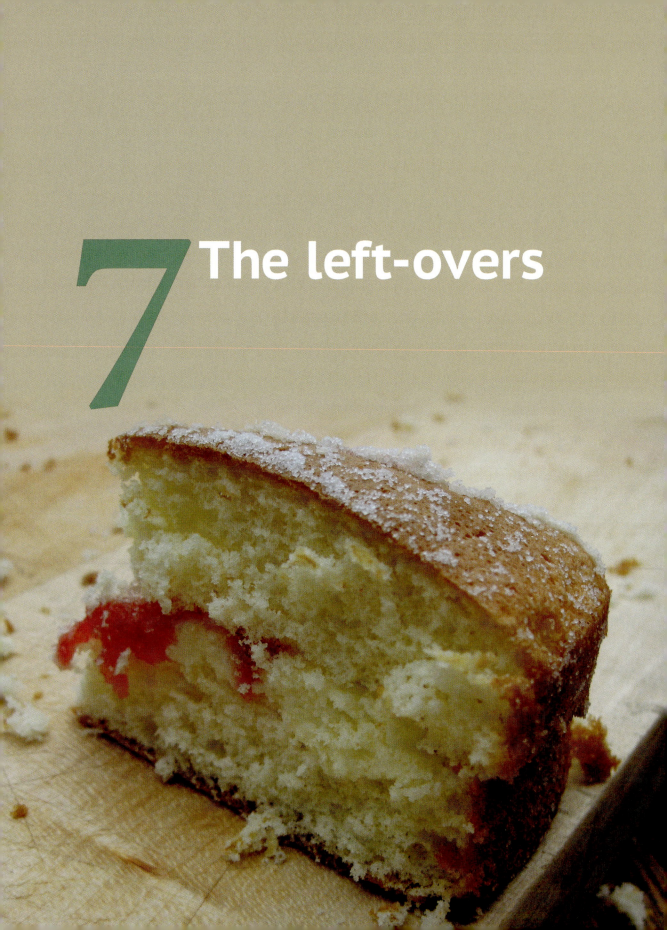

7 The left-overs

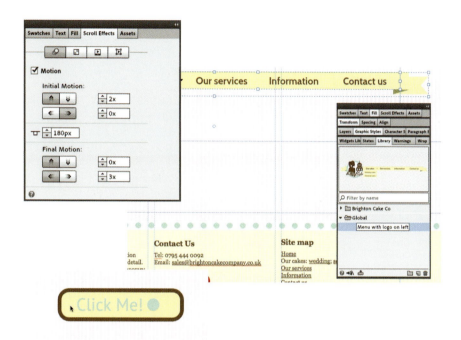

Many of the features in the current version of Muse came in too late to use, or didn't fit in to the design of the example site. This final chapter is a mixture of more advanced techniques and demonstrations of the most important features that didn't make it into the main sections.

The left-overs
An alternate navigation bar

At the beginning of the book we encountered a problem when setting up the main navigation menu. Initially, I wanted the site logo in the middle, the idea was to represent the ribbon around a cake with a centerpiece. This caused problems with the way the site loaded its pages, so I opted to alter the design. Here we'll look at a method of changing the layout of the menu without affecting the sitemap.

Add a new master page

We'll begin by creating a duplicate of the master page. This way we don't affect the current layout whilst we're working. We'll also be able to quickly switch between the layouts later.

Right-click the master page on the site plan. Select **Duplicate Page**. Rename the copy B-Master.

Create a dummy page

Create a new page between *Our Services* and *Information*. Name this page *Home Icon*. The name is not really relevant as it will be covered but it needs to space out the menu items enough to accommodate the logo without it overlapping the labels.

▶ Since this is only a placeholder, we don't need to upload the page itself. Right-click the page thumbnail. Uncheck the **Export Page** item. We can also remove its hyperlink by selecting the option: **Include Page without Hyperlink**.

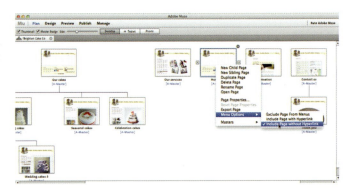

▶ Now we can edit the page template. Open the *B-Master* page in **Design mode**. Use the **Selection tool** to move the logo into the center of the page; hold **Shift** to constrain the horizontal movement.

▶ Click the menu to select it. Drag the left handle over to align with the left page content guide. As we do, the menu spacing expands to fit the space. The dummy page item is hidden beneath as we had arranged the logo to appear above the other page elements when we first created the menu.

▶ Once we've previewed the new menu design to make sure it works we can apply the master to the pages. There are a couple of ways to do this: we can drag the *B-Master* thumbnail onto the page thumbnail or right-click the page thumbnail and select from the **Masters** sub-menu. The pages update as we do so.

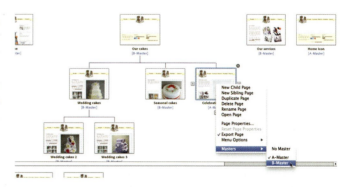

You're still the master

Working with multiple master pages is great for trying out different layouts. Remember to update the 404 page if you stick with the change. If we later decide to return to the first master page then we'll need to remove the placeholder page, as it will show up in the original menu layout. Rather than deleting it, set its menu option to **Exclude from Menus**.

The left-overs

Working with scroll effects

One of the major features in Muse is called scroll effects. Scroll effects allow you to make items move and have items moving independent of one another and at different speeds in relation to the speed the page is being scrolled. This gives us a huge amount of scope for creating interactive design elements and effects. In this section we'll be looking at the concept behind scroll effects and some of their practical uses.

The Scroll Effects panel

Object movement and other effects are controlled using the **Scroll Effects panel**; fill settings are handled individually. There are four separate sections in the panel. The first is for motion (shown here), the second allows us to control the object's opacity. The third section is used to control slideshow content. The last section is for integrating Adobe Edge Animations, where the scroll motion controls the animation content to a limited extent.

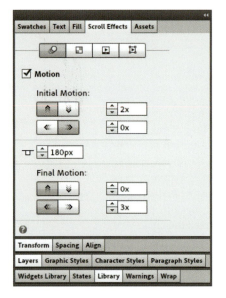

The Scroll Effects panel determines how objects interact with the page as it scrolls.

- **Initial Motion**: this determines the behaviour of the object before the page has scrolled past the key position. There are four arrows to set the movement direction. Each direction block has a value to its right. This controls the speed in relation to the page scroll. A value of 1x means the object moves at the same speed as the scroll movement. Setting a value lower than 1x means the movement will be slower, e.g. 0.5x will move at half the speed of the page scroll. Similarly, setting a value higher than 1 will mean the object moves faster than the scroll: 2x being twice that of the scroll movement. A value of 0 means the object will be fixed in position and does not move as the page scrolls.

- **Key position** (not labeled): this defines the actual position on the page which differentiates the settings in the Initial Motion from the settings applied in the Final Motion. In other words its relative position in the **Design mode**. We can set the value numerically here in the panel

or visually by dragging the T-Handle guide on the page. For example, if we set the value to **180px**, the object will move at the speed and direction defined by the **Initial Motion** setting to arrive at that position when the key position is scrolled to the top of the browser window (see illustration on the facing page). Since the speed setting is constant, the higher the speed setting, the further away from the key position our object begins. To move it off the visible portion of the page here would require us to increase the scroll speed.

- **Final Motion**: this determines the behaviour of the object after the page reaches and scrolls past the key position. The settings are applied in the same way as the Initial Motion.

Scroll effect mechanics

This is a basic example to demonstrate the mechanics of scroll motion. The square has been given the motion settings shown on the opposite page. The key position and the object's position on the page have been marked with guides and text. Note the T-handle guide line extending up to the 180px marker.

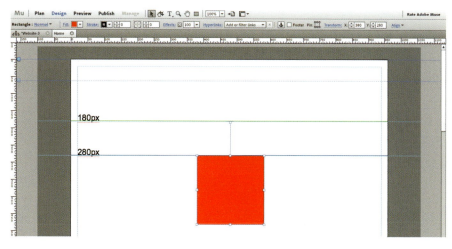

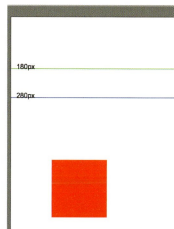

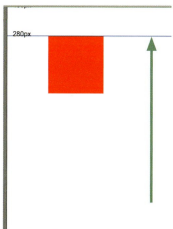

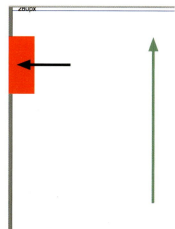

When previewed in the browser, the square is displayed offset from its starting position. This is roughly twice the distance, as we have set the speed to 2x the scroll speed.

As we scroll down the page, the square moves up at twice the speed of the scroll. When the key position marker is at the top of the browser, the square reaches its set position.

Once we begin to scroll past the key position, the Final Motion setting comes into effect, in this case, the box moves over to the left at three times the scroll speed.

7 The left-overs

Create a 'sticky' menu

Normally, when the page is scrolled up, the header content, which includes the Menu widget, disappears off the screen. Using scroll effects, we can create a menu that starts to scroll off the page but sticks to the browser window when it reaches the top. This is useful if we have a large header that we don't want taking up space.

We'll begin by creating a new master based on the central logo version of the menu. Right-click the *B-Master* thumbnail. Select **Duplicate Page**. Name this *C-Master*.

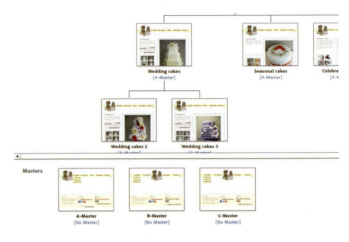

▶ We need to make some changes to the menu. Open the new master page in design mode. Go to the **Layers panel**. Click the **New Layer** icon at the bottom. Name the layer *Menu*. Make sure it's at the top of the stack as we need it to display above the rest of the site content.

▶ We'll group the menu and the ribbon image together. This makes it easier to have them scrolling in unison. Grab the **Selection tool**. Click and drag a selection over the right edge of the ribbon so it picks up the end of the *Contact Us* menu entry.

Go to the **Object** menu. Select **Group** (keyboard shortcut **Cmd+G**/**Ctrl+G**). Don't worry that the menu is now in front of the logo, we'll sort that out next.

▶ Right-click the new grouped object to display the menu and choose the option **Move to Layer**. Select *Menu*. Now select the logo image frame and move that to the menu layer. The logo now appears above menu.

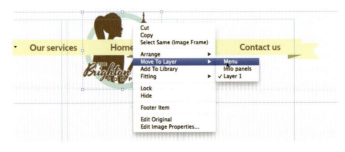

▸Make sure the menu group is the active object. Go over to the **Scroll Effects panel**. Enable the **Motion** checkbox.

We want the menu to travel up at the same speed as the page scroll, so we'll set the initial motion to **up** and its speed to **1x**; make sure the horizontal movement is set to **0x**. As the menu needs to stop when it hits the top of the browser, the **Key Position** needs to be the same as the top of the menu itself. Drag the T-handle down to the top of the group's frame, or set the value numerically, in this case, it's **72px**.

Lastly, we need to freeze the menu in position at the top of the window, to do this we set the **Final Motion** values to **0x**.

▸The master page currently isn't tall enough to scroll, which is necessary for scroll effects to work. Go back to the **Plan mode**. Create a new page named *Scroll test* based on the *C-Master* page. Set the **Menu Option** to **Exclude Page From Menus**.

Open the Page Properties. Set the **Min Height** value to **2000px**. This will ensure there is plenty of space to scroll the page without needing to add content to space it out. Click **OK** to apply the setting.

▸Open the new page in **Design mode**. We don't see any change, apart from the footer no longer being visible.

When we test the page in **Preview mode** and start scrolling down, the menu moves to the top of the browser window with the other page content. When the top of the menu widget (which is also the key position) reaches the top of the browser window, it stops. If we continue scrolling the logo disappears, revealing the *Home* link beneath. If we scroll back up, the logo moves back into place and the menu moves down, stopping at its initial location.

7 The left-overs

Flying items onto the page

We saw how we can use scroll effects to recede the menu to give us more page space. We can also use it to fly page items onto the page to add interactivity to the design.

   To demonstrate this, I've imported some of the original site content to the *Scroll test* page. The home page content is static, as it's intended to be seen at the start. Below it, I've pasted in the content from the *Our Services* page. We'll use different scroll effects to control how the elements are displayed.

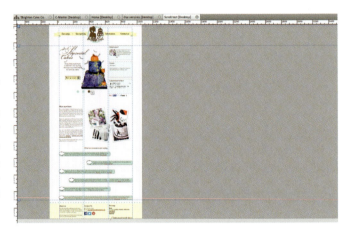

▶We'll start by having the four images moving into position: the top row will drop down, the bottom row will emerge from the right side of the page.

   Select the top-left image. Go to the **Scroll Effects panel**. Enable the motion checkbox. Click the down directional arrow. Set the speed to **3x**.

▶The images need to be in place before the section heading is too far up in the browser. Remember that the menu is now fixed at this point, so we need to take that into account. We can use the static page elements as a cue here.

   Drag a **Horizontal guide** down from the ruler to sit at the top of the social media buttons. Make a note of the Y position, it's **830px** in the example. Set the **Key Position** value to match; its T-Handle will now be resting level with the guide.

   The image needs to continue scrolling with the page once it's in position, so we can leave the default setting for **Final Motion** as **Up** at **1x** speed.

▶ Click the top-right image. Enable motion. Set everything the same as the previous image, apart from the **Initial Motion** speed. Set this to **8x**. This will drop the image down faster than the left side but it will still arrive at the same time. This gives the animation a bit of variety.

▶ Now for the bottom row of images. Select the bottom-left image. Enable scroll motion. This time set the **Initial Motion** direction to **Left** at **3x** speed. We'll have the images hitting their final positions slightly later than the top row. Set the **Key Position** to **850px**. The **Final Motion** setting remains at its default of upward motion at **1x** speed.

▶ Select the bottom-right image. This time we'll alter the way it travels. The previous image will slide in diagonally, as the page is moving up at the same time as the object is moving horizontally. To have the image slide in at 90° we need to alter the **Initial Motion** slightly. Set the horizontal movement to **Left** at **8x**, to be different from the previous image. Set the vertical movement to **Up** at **0.5x** speed. This will match the speed of the scroll, keeping the movement more or less level. The remainder of the settings are the same as before.

What our customers are saying

Birthday cakes, they were fantastic and the highlight of our ...rward to many more to eat. *Archie & Millie (Southwick)*

Move in new directions

We can mix the direction and speed of the motion to create different effects based on the scroll of the page. With a little experimentation, objects can be set to swoop in and out with dramatic arcs. The only thing lacking is the ability to control the acceleration of the movement, which would give us even more scope in the design.

7 The left-overs

Change an item's opacity

We just saw how we can use scroll effects to move items on a page, in this section we'll look at how the opacity of items can be changed as the page moves.

Select the text item *What our customers are saying*. Go to the **Scroll Effects panel**. Click the second button to open the Opacity controls; check the **Opacity** checkbox to enable them. As with the motion control settings, we see the T-Handle extending away from the text frame.

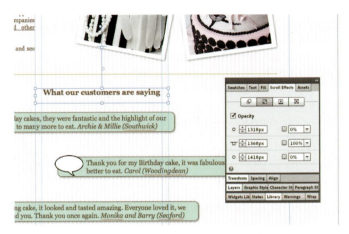

▶ The settings are similar to those of the motion panel. Instead of direction and speed, however, we have position and percentage fields. The first setting is for the initial opacity of the object. By default this is 0%, so when the page is previewed, the text frame is hidden.

Just as we have the **Key Position** setting to define the final position for scroll motion, the key setting here determines the object's opacity when the value we set is at the top of the browser: 100% in the example. The second opacity setting controls the visibility of the object as we scroll past the key position.

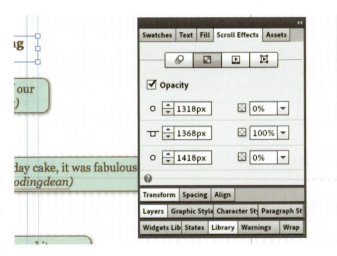

▶ Like scroll motion, we need to plan where on the page our objects will be at their full visibility. In this example, they'll be fading in at the bottom of the page. Although the layout of the settings in the panel suggests we set the initial opacity first, I find it's best to set the key position then adjust the start and finish opacity afterward.

Set the page at the position we want the text to be fully visible. Drag the **Key Position guide** to the top of the window. In this case, it's just below the images in the slideshow. Make sure the key position opacity value is **100%**.

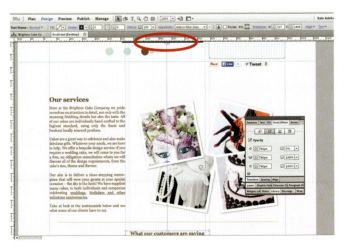

▶ The next step is to set the initial opacity. This needs to remain at 0%. The distance from the key position determines the speed at which the transition occurs, the greater the amount, the longer the object takes to fade in/out and vice versa.

Drag the **Fade Position 1** guide of the T-handle up, I've set it to **660px**, which gives a short but noticeable fade. If you're applying the same transition to several items, it's always a good idea to make the distances easier to calculate.

▶ The second opacity guide sets the visibility of the object after reaching the key position. We want it to remain at 100% so make sure this is the current value. Since there's no transition required, we can set the position of the second guide to the same value as the key position, **760px** in the example.

▶ Now to set the fade for the comment boxes. Select the top-most box. Move it into the position we want it at 100% opacity. Adjust the settings as before, using a **100px** fade transition. We could set the remaining boxes by eye but since they're uniformly spaced, we simply need to use the settings from the first, adding the difference, **106px** in this case, to the key position and off-setting the initial opacity by **-100px**. The second opacity setting will be the same as the key for each in this example.

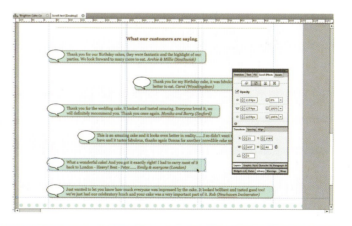

Position is everything

It's important to take the browser window's height into account whenever you're using scroll effects, especially in the lower portions of the page. Here, for example, with the Muse application frame at its current dimensions, the objects fade in just as they emerge at the bottom of the window. If we were to stretch the window to twice its current height, however, the objects would only begin to appear when they were roughly half-way up the page. Conversely, if we were to view the page in a shorter window, we might not see the effect at all. We also need to have a sufficient amount of space below to ensure all the objects' key positions reach the top, otherwise they may only appear partially or not at all.

7 The left-overs
Setting up Google Analytics

Although Muse Dashboard has its own site statistics pages, if you're publishing to a third-party host, or just want an alternative, you'll need to use a different strategy for tracking page metrics. The most popular system is Google Analytics, of course. In this section we'll look at how to go about configuring the site to use an existing Google account. If you don't already have an account set up, information for creating one can be found here: *http://www.google.com/analytics*.

Create a new property

To set up our site for analytics, we need to create a new profile (known as a property) with your Analytics account. To do this, go to the **Admin** section, select the account to create the site under, in the example it's *Client sites*. Click **Select a property** then **Create new property**.

Set the tracking type

The next part of the setup is to define the type of tracking and the site details. Make sure the Website property is highlighted. At the time of writing, *Universal Analytics* is still in beta, so we'll go with the *Classic* version here. This still offers everything we need to be able to track our site visitors. We can always change it at a later date.

Add the site details

The next section is for the name of the site. This is how it's identified in the list of sites in the Analytics account, *Brighton Cake Company* here. Next is the site URL. This would normally be the primary address. I'm using the Muse trial site address in the example as the company's domain name has not yet transferred over. We'll set the *Industry Category* to *Food and Drink*. Finally we have the Reporting Time Zone. I've set it to *United Kingdom* as the company is based here.

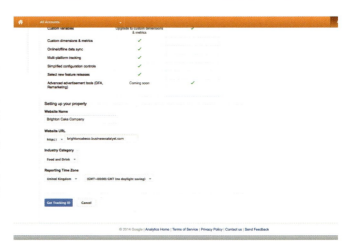

Create a tracking ID

Take a moment to check the settings are correct. Click the **Get Tracking ID** button. This brings us to a new page. We don't need to change anything at the top of the page, we're only concerned with the block of code at the bottom. Click inside the box to highlight it. Go to **Edit > Copy** or press **Cmd+C/Ctrl+C** to store a copy on the clipboard.

Set up the tracking code

Go back to Muse. Open the **Plan mode**. Right-click the *A-Master* page. Select **Page Properties.** Click the **Metadata** tab. Right-click inside the *HTML for <head>* window. Select **Paste** (or press **Cmd+V/Ctrl+V**) to paste the copied code. Click **OK**.

This applies the code to every page with the currently selected master page. Remember to do the same for the alternate master pages as well.

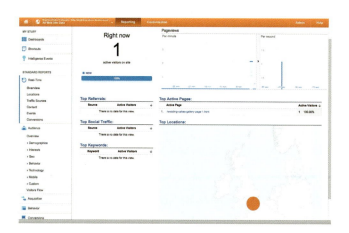

Test the account

Now that the code is in place we can republish the site. It will take time to show up a full set of statistics, of course.

To demonstrate that it's already doing its job, I took a snapshot of the real-time monitor in the *Reporting* section of Analytics, just after publishing the site. We can see that there's one active visitor (that's me) and that two pages have been viewed, along with my location.

7 The left-overs
Creating a State Button

In this section we'll be looking at another recent feature in Muse: the State Button widget. States can only be applied to a single element, so if we create a button with a graphic background and text, although the links go to the same place, the rollover state for the background and text are independent of each other; we'll either see the text change, or the background, depending on where the cursor is. The State Button acts as a container; we can drag a group of items, each with their own rollover states, into the widget. When we move the cursor onto the button, all the object's states change in unison.

Use a scratch page

We'll start by creating a scratch page. Go to the site plan. Create a new page named *Scratch*. Right-click its thumbnail. Deselect **Publish Page**. Select **Exclude From Menus**. We'll use the *A-Master* template here.

Create a composite button

Open the scratch page. Grab the **Rectangle tool**. Draw out a rectangle. Set its Fill color to *Warm Yellow*. Set a **10px** Stroke. Enable rounded corners at a **Radius** of **30px**. Set the Stroke color to *Mint Green*. This will be the basis of our button.

Switch to the **Text tool**. Draw out a text frame inside the button so it fits just inside the stroke. Set the font to PT Sans regular. Set the color to *Chocolate Brown*. Type in *Click Me!*. Now increase the size to fit the button. In this example, it's **45px**.

Create a new rectangle to the right of the text. Hold the **Shift** key to constrain the shape to a square. Drag it out to match the height of the text. Set the color to *Chocolate Brown*. Remove the stroke. Set the **Corner Radius** to its maximum of **100**. This turns the square to a circle.

190

▶ That's the button graphic completed. Now we'll set the Rollover states for each element. Click the background rectangle. Go to the **States panel**. Select the Rollover state. Change the Stroke color to *Chocolate Brown*.

The Mouse Down state updates automatically to match the settings of the Rollover state. Leave the Active state settings as is.

▶ Click the text frame. Select its Rollover state. Change the color to *Mint Green*. Now do the same for the circle.

When we preview the page, we see different results, depending on the placement of the cursor on the button.

Add the State widget

Go to the **Composition** section of the **Widgets Library**. Drag the **State Button** widget over to the page. Start by scaling it up to just larger than our button.

▶ First we need to remove the placeholder content. Click the circle. Press **Delete** or **Backspace**. Do the same for the text.

Go to the **States panel**, make sure the Normal state is selected. Change the Fill color to *None*. Select the Rollover state. Click the **Trash** icon to clear the remaining states.

Create the combined item

The widget is not visible but the State Button container is still where we left it. Select all the items in our button. Don't group them, though. Drag them down onto the widget, its frame will highlight as we move over it. Release the mouse to drop them into the state widget container. When previewed, all the items change in unison.

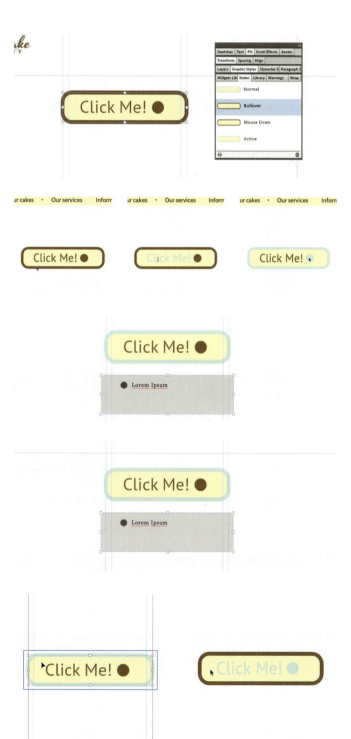

7 The left-overs
Working with Muse Libraries

Earlier in the book, we briefly looked at the Library panel and its ability to store entire groups of design elements as a single entity, in order to reuse them later. This is incredibly useful, of course, but there is a whole lot more to the Library and the way we can use the items we store there. In this section we'll create a truly universal library item that can be set to adapt to the look of the site its placed in. We'll also see how items can be shared and imported, both privately and publicly.

Preparing the library item

We'll use the button we created in the previous section. Before we start, we'll need to make some changes. Go to the **Swatches panel**. Right-click the *Chocolate Brown* color preset. Select **Duplicate Swatch** to create a copy. Do the same for the *Mint Green* and *Warm Yellow* presets.

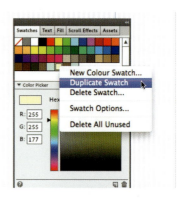

▶ Double-click the duplicate *Warm Yellow* swatch to open the **Swatch Options** dialog. Rename the swatch *Color 1*. Click **OK** to apply the change. Do the same for the *Mint Green* and *Chocolate Brown* copies, naming them *Color 2* and *Color 3* respectively.

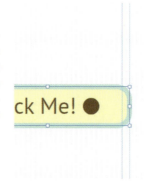

▶ Now we need to change the colors in the button to the new presets we created. The reason for this will become apparent later in the section.

Click through the elements, changing the background, stroke and text colors to use the swatches named *Color 1*, *Color 2*, and *Color 3*. Remember to reset the color swatches for the button's states, too.

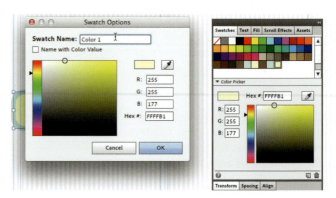

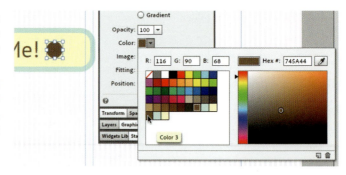

▶Click the button background to make it the active object. Go to the **Graphic Styles panel**. Create a new style named *Button Lozenge*. Note the style settings showing the new colors we applied. Do the same for the circle item, name it *Button Circle*.

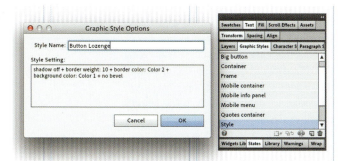

▶Select the text item. Go to the **Paragraph Styles panel**. Create a new style named *Button Text*. Again, we see the new color preset in the settings.

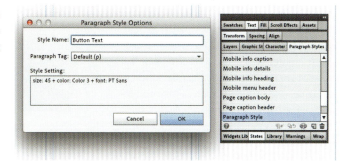

Add to the library

▶Go to the **Library panel**. Click the **Create folder** button. Name it *Buttons*. Click the button object to select it. Press **Esc** to make sure the active item is the State Button by referring to the Selection Indicator.

Highlight the folder we created. Now click the **Add selected item(s)** icon to add it into the library. Name it *Lozenge Button*. It's now stored in the buttons folder.

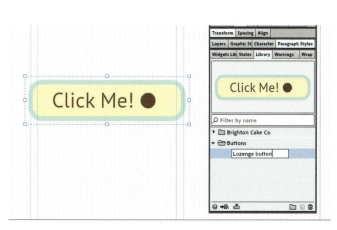

Creating your library structure

If there are currently no items in the Library, adding a new item will automatically create a parent folder to contain it. This will be named *Untitled*, as will the new item within it. Both can be renamed, of course. Once the library has one or more folders, we see a list in the sub-menu so we can choose the destination. If we don't want to add the item to any of the existing folders, we must create a new folder beforehand.

7 The left-overs

Adaptive library items

The true power of library items is the ability to reuse them in new sites. Go to **File > New Site** (**Cmd+N/Ctrl+N**). Click **OK** to accept the default settings. Open the *Home* page in Design mode. If we look at the **Library panel** we see both the cake company folder and the *Buttons* folder we just created.

▶ To demonstrate how library items can adapt, we'll create a color scheme for our new site. Go to the **Swatches panel**. Pick a warm orange. Click the **Add swatch** icon. Open its options dialog. Name it *Color 1*, as we did before. Ensure the name is exactly the same, case included, as the swatch name we assigned on the main site.

Create two more, a fiery orange for *Color 2* and finally a midnight blue for *Color 3*.

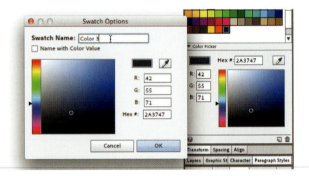

▶ Grab the **Text tool**. Draw out a text frame on the page. Set the font to something other than the one used for the original button, I've used the web font *Source Sans Pro light*. Set the size to **45px**. Set the color to *Color 3*.

Create a new paragraph style. Name it *Button Text,* again making sure it matches the name we used for the button exactly. The sample text frame can be deleted.

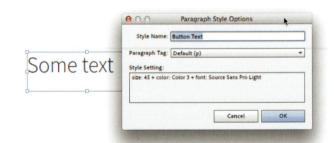

▶ Go back to the **Library panel**. Drag the *Lozenge button* over to the page. Although it looks the same in the library, as soon as we place it down, its colors and type face change to use the font and color attributes that are specific to the current site.

As long as we maintain a naming convention from site to site, the button will automatically adapt to the scheme. With this on board we have a huge scope for making reusable site assets.

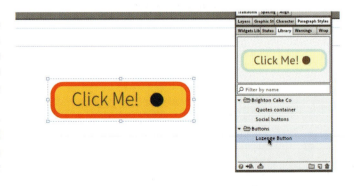

194

Exporting and importing

Library items can be exported as packaged files to share with other people, and as a backup. Highlight the folder or individual asset you want to export. Click the **Export selected item(s) as a Muse Library** icon. The **Export Library Items** dialog box appears. The default file name is always the parent folder, regardless of whether we choose a single item or the entire folder.

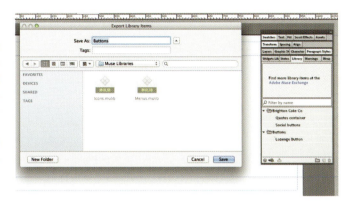

▶ To open a library item in Muse, we can either double-click the file – the suffix is *.mulib* and is associated with Muse – or click the **Import Muse library** icon. Here I've imported a library I downloaded from the *Muse Exchange* page.

Each item is self-contained, retaining its color palette and styles. If any of these match those of the destination, they'll be overridden, just like the behaviour we saw with the button.

Library items: caveat

Library items can contain bitmap images as well as shapes and text, of course. It's important to note that the source image files themselves won't be included in the export file by default. If we look at the **Assets panel** we see that all the components of the icon are missing. Although this will not affect the site when it's published, as Muse uses the cached versions. It does mean that the images cannot be edited by the recipient.

Make your libraries self-supporting

To get around the problem of missing images, we can either send the originals separately, or we can embed them into the asset; this must be done before it's added to the library. To embed an asset, go to the **Assets panel**, right-click the asset's entry. Select **Embed link**. This instructs Muse to save the original asset, both inside the saved site file and any subsequent library exports. This will increase the size of the resulting files, of course. In some cases they will be enormous, if the files are scaled down from much larger images. So care must be taken if they are destined to be sent to other people.

Index

Index